An Anthology of
New (American) Poets

An
Anthology
of New
(American)
Poets

edited by
Lisa Jarnot
Leonard Schwartz
and
Chris Stroffolino

Talisman House, Publishers
Jersey City, New Jersey

Published in the United States of America by
Talisman House, Publishers
P.O. Box 3157
Jersey City, New Jersey 07303-3157

Manufactured in the United Sates of America
Printed on acid-free paper
Cover art: Carol Goebel, "Arching Flyer", Steel, 33" x 26" X 9", 1966;
Courtesy Denise Bibro Fine Art, New York, NY; Photo: Sarah Lewis

Library of Congress Cataloging-in-Publication Data

An anthology of new (American) poets / edited by Lisa Jarnot, Leonard
Schwartz, and Chris Stroffolino.
　　p.　　cm.
　　ISBN 1-883689-62-7 (cloth : alk. paper). – ISBN 1-883689-61-9
(pbk. : alk. paper)
　　1. American poetry. 2. American poetry–20th century.
I. Jarnot, Lisa, 1967- . II. Schwartz, Leonard, 1963- .
III. Stroffolino, Chris.
PS586.A59　1998 JUN 0 1 1998
811'.5408–dc21　　　　　　　　　　　　　　　　　　97-50296
　　　　　　　　　　　　　　　　　　　　　　　　　　　　　　　CIP

Acknowledgments: Permission to print copyright material is acknowledged gratefully
here and on the following two pages, which are hereby declared to be part of the copyright
page: Brenda Coulas, "Eat" from *Early Films* (Rodent Press, 1996). Copyright © 1996 by
Brenda Coultas. Reprinted with the permission of the author. • Jordan Davis: "A Little
Gold Book" from *A Little Gold Book* (Golden, 1995). Copyright © 1995 by Jordan Davis.
Reprinted with the permission of the author. • Thomas Sayers Ellis: "A Baptist Beat" from
The Good Junk, in *Take Three: AGNI New Poets Series* (Graywolf Press, 1996). Copyright ©
1996 by Thomas Sayers Ellis. Reprinted with the permission of the author. • Benjamin
Friedlander: "Ah but who emptied . . ." from *Myth* (Phobics, 1989). Copyright © 1989 by
Benjamin Friedlander. Reprinted with the permission of the author. – "Nature" from
Anterior Future (Meow Press, 1993). Copyright © 1993 by Benjamin Friedlander. Reprinted
with the permission of the author. • Peter Gizzi: "Ding Repair," "A Textbook of Chivalry,"
"At Earth" from *Artificial Heart* (Providence: Burning Deck, 1998). Copyright © 1998 by
Peter Gizzi. Reprinted with the permission of the author. – "Life Continues," "News at
Eleven," "Deus ex Machina" from *Periplum* (Penngrove, CA: Avec Books, 1992). Copyright
© 1992 by Peter Gizzi. Reprinted with the permission of the author. – "Poem for John
Wieners" from *Hours of the Book* (Canary Islands: Zasterle Press, 1994). Copyright © 1994

• Thomas Sayers Ellis: "Zapruder" (*Ploughshares*), "Spellbound" (*Graham House Review*), "Slow Fade to Black" (*Ploughshares*), "Parliament/Funkadelic" (*Grand Street*), "Sir Nose D'VoidofFunk" (*AGNI Document Series*), "A Psychoalphadisco-betabioaquadoloop" (*Callaloo*) • Benjamin Friedlander: "Insomnia" (*AQL*), "Christ" (*tel-net*), "Little Wing" (*tel-net*), "The Soul / Is This Liberal Falling Away" (*Dark Ages Clasp the Daisy Root*) • Yuri (Riq) Hospodar: "Dwelling On/In" (*Painted Bridge Quarterly*) • Candace Kaucher: "Ex Post Facto God" (*6ix*) • Bill Luoma: "Phainetai Moi (Sappho)" (*Dark Ages Clasp the Daisy Root*), "Hoi Men Hippeon Straton (Sappho)" (*Dark Ages Clasp the Daisy Root*), "Wings of Love (Simias)" (*Dark Ages Clasp the Daisy Root*), "Egg (Simias)" (*Letterbox*), "Vanilla" (*The Impercipient*), "Swing" (*The Impercipient*) • Kimberly Lyons: "Eon" (*Mass Ave.*) • Mark Nowak: "How shall I praise you . . ." (*Northwest Review*, 31.1 [1993]), reprinted with the permission of the editors of *Northwest Review*; "The calendar of you . . ."(*The Midwest Quarterly* 36.4 [1995]), reprinted with the permission of The Midwest Quarterly • "Stworzenie" (*Five Fingers Review*), "The sun rises each morning simply . . ." (*Five Fingers Review*), "The house or hand . . ." (*Five Fingers Review*), "We have by now . . ." (*First Intensity*), "Off-shore, / even if there was . . ." (*Talisman*) • Hoa Nguyen: "Surrogate Houses" (*Explosive*), "Shred" (*Dale's Younger Poets*), "Walk" (*Gas*), "Answer" (*Gas*), "Play" (*Gas*), "Bare" (*Open 24 Hours*), "Here" (*Open 24 Hours*) • Heather Ramsdell: "Where Things of a Kind" (*Talisman*), "Bridge Segment" (*Sulfur*) • Pam Rehm: "A Trivial Pursuit" (*LUNG*), "The Humiliation of the Valley" (*apex of the M*) • Susan M. Schultz: "The Lost Country" (*RIF/t*; #I, *Talisman*; #IX, *Kaimana*). "Mothers and Dinosaurs, Inc." (*New American Writing*), "The Philosopher's Child" (*Verse*), "Drive ME" (*Denver Quarterly*) • Elio Schneeman: "July" (*The World*) • Leonard Schwartz: "Pages from an Imaginary Escape" (*First Intensity*) • Chris Stroffolino: "Allowance Money That is Death to You" (*Letterbox*), "Fragile Blonde" (*Object*), "Fish Story" (*American Letters and Commentary*) • Edwin Torres: "A Morir Soñando — To Die Dreaming..." (*Long Shot*), "A Page from the Flictionary of Deafeningition" (*The World*) • • • The following works are published here for the first time: Beth Anderson: "Float and Land," "Arrangements" • Lee Ann Brown: "Menage a deux," "May Visitation," "My Epithalamion," "The Current Scene," "The Current Scene Continued Which I Love to See," "Open Sez Me (T&G)," "Procrastination Sonnet," "Catullus Couch" • Brenda Coultas: "My Life and My Death," "An Installation Piece," "The Three Men" • Jordan Davis: "By the Ruins," "Dying To," "The Loan" • Thomas Sayers Ellis: "Houston Summit (1976)" • Drew Gardner: "Passive Fire," "The Bridge," "Partials," "Heading South," "Cell Walk," "The Source Log" • Yuri (Riq) Hospodar: "Spiritual," "The Clarified Moose," "Beatrice Has Left the Building" • Garrett Kalleberg: "The New Gate," "Inside-of-the-Body Test" • Candace Kaucher: "Swallowed Opinions But Good Ones," "Virginibus Puerisque," "Chloroforms," "There Is Only So Much Space in Time," "Molecular Viscosity," "Perceptual Distance," "Ode Through Gravity to Space" • Bill Luoma, "Altar (Besantius)" • Kimberly Lyons: "Millefleur" • Jeffrey McDaniel: "The Quiet World," "Opposites Attack" • Claire Needell: "Space Remains," "Another, Being," "But for Now," "Another and Another," "Another One," "View," "In These Particulars," "Feathers," "Patterns of Identification," "Frame by Frame," "To Witness to Hunt," "Here and There" • Mark Nowak: *"Zwiastowanie,"* "In the northern range in the mountains . . . ," *"(Grzech Pierworodny . . ."* • Heather Ramsdell: "Bright Receding" • Pam Rehm: "November Testament" • Eleni Sikelianos: "Thus, Speak the Chromograph," "J(oy)'s the Aim (essay)," "In a Pre-Raphaelite Light," "The Decameron," "The Brambles of Cavalry (Quamash)," "Poem (My eye can't fix you . . .)," from *Unbridled* • Juliana Spahr: "spiderwasp / or / literary criticism" • Edwin Torres: "Tightrope Curves Across Equator," "Bizzarro World Adrift"

To the Memory
of
Elio Schneeman

Contents

ix

An Anthology of
New (American) Poets

Preface

From the beginning of this project, Leonard Schwartz, Chris Stroffolino, and I knew that we would face certain difficulties in preparing such a book, but at the same time we were eager to bring our various ideas to the table, and to attempt to learn something about our own generation. What we have shared as editors is a respect for a wide range of traditions of writing, even though our own aesthetic values vary significantly. What we agreed upon during our first meeting was that this book should include approximately 35 writers whose work was a process of a synthesis, rather than an extension of any one of the experimental writings which have taken place in the United States and elsewhere in the past. All of the writers included in this collection were born between 1958 and 1973; most were born in the 1960s. Most of them have also published a first book of poetry.

The poetry included in this anthology presents a cross-section of what we saw as a very large group of young writers scattered across the United States. It is our hope that readers of this book will recognize the flaws and omissions, and that these will be amended by another group of anthologists in the not so distant future. There were several factors that we considered in our final selections for this volume. Overall, we attempted to include writers of as diverse a geography as possible and we attempted to look beyond the predictable alignments of writers to institutions of higher learning. At the same time we discovered that many young poets were huddling around major metropolitan areas, and we also found that many writers inevitably had passed through or lived on the periphery of an academic community, the most obvious being Brown University's M.F.A. program, the State University of New York at Buffalo's Poetics program, the Naropa Institute's Jack Kerouac School of Disembodied Poetics, Bard College, and New College of California. But what became most evident in the process was that poets in their early thirties in the United States were working on similar projects, whether or not they had actually interacted with each other in person. There are several diverse groupings of experimental writers in North America, and while the boundaries of their physical spaces may be clear, the boundaries of their work are much less rigid. What all of these writers share, beyond their marginalization from mainstream literary culture, are the facts of the world into which they were born.

Coming of age in the 1970s and 1980s meant witnessing the fragmentation and disintegration of the Left in the United States. It meant seeing the country's loss of economic hegemony and subsequent xenophobic internal and international policies. It meant, in general, wading through the alienation of commodity culture, the grief of an AIDS epidemic, and the beginning of the end of a liveable global ecosystem. What is surprising is to come out of such circumstances of childhood into life as a poet and to again embrace the world with some determination to communicate candidly, with hope, and with urgency. The communication that rings through these pages is one of a keen desire for social interaction, an openness to diversity of experiment, and an earnestness in the intellectual and philosophical pursuits that one might associate with those who call their craft poetry. This work is not without cynicism, it's not without confusion, and it's not without a great mistrust for the structures of the body politic or the body poetic. However, it is filled with a new charge — a renewed interest in the continuity of traditions of writing, a critique of the dire economic and social conditions which surround us, and a sincere approach to the fact that we have much to learn from each other and from our individual poetical practices. Many of us have opted to move in different directions aesthetically, variously being influenced by the Black Mountain School, the Beats, the New York School, and the Language School. We have also taken in the work of the great innovators of experimentation throughout history, simultaneously pausing to consider the "new" — from electronic multimedia venues to hip hop. We are a generation critically aware that as Allen Ginsberg said in 1966, "almost all our language has been taxed by war." And perhaps what we share the most at this moment is an unspoken thought that John Cage is right when he tells us that language is something "that you have to use in practical ways, for survival."

Lisa Jarnot
1 August 1997

Beth Anderson

ARRANGEMENTS

It's a small dream, that of silence   and dry, how to use
mayhap   Another desert entered the landscape
and left us with this one, asking what remains
aside from a ponderous leaf flying and *siren* the verb

Finally people moved
though they were understood as part of the architecture
or the poise this evokes, hand just so
and others appended   In choreography
wished into then out of sync
existence gathered and unraveled in a number of beats
resembling the syllabic

Relish the initiate sounds
and what whey will become when they leave
Reminisce with me, for we once sprang into motion
while famished   heraldry across one rough stone
kept us going when the spurious wind declared itself
and the harvest went bad while still in the ground

This has always been a familiar passage
We couldn't claim ourselves from the lineup but did desist
en masse we did one thing we wanted
but that's another key   and the softest part of the animal
Fiction beckons from outside as if by leaving
at least rerouting   punctuation would give pleasure

From pews in which one sat and lost
another followed and thus association bore
the seconds we called out   wished again for another alphabet
larger than the boy on the stoop

and an alumnus darting across the screen
who apprized us that false dawn is out of books, is dried
to hang from a beam and hung mindlessly in
a pattern unlike its rhyme   Our plan became irrelevant
like music discharged from a window or the gesture made
in response   hoping to subsist on idolatry and larkspur
a series so smooth made the leap easy to take

EVIDENCE

The hollows   the metal details made to support and confine
Like fog covering parts of buildings some chronicles
can be foreseen while others are surprises, an assembly of scents
camouflaging one another   Abrupt   the grey air
the seams which show the making of some object rendered vague

Each time we cross a river I try to name it
but cannot envision a map of these routes, crisscrossing
what should be a scripted life   No longer simply that
which is pulled from a drawer prior to travel
instituting *memory* as a byword, instead

my figure   imagined   is the equivalent of a wet clothesline
to the left, of an abandoned smokestack further up
the glimpsed conglomerate   Some tissue ripples as a form of notation
and sawdust floats off   Then, we roamed the city
on determined feet, unveiled skills seldom applied

No motion suffices   Nothing edible appeals   In small cavities
scattered along the coast, swathed with what storms carry in
the script transfigures pressure into tongues
shapes of sentences in illuminated sand
inspired by wind and fauna and shocked into form by voice

Who can tell what holds together layers of wood
or who painted one ragged metal sheet with the word *end*?
Around the house are drums to hold oil and the planning of
what has been identified as a reasonable day   This lushness
suits its own setting, including time

away from which you have temporarily stepped   as a terrified animal
scuttles against the house's edge, disrupting
those rich wheels called love   If only the spokes
were of metal or the space beneath the stairway empty
then our stitches could be removed   a surreality in the proper room

No flat spaces   Some parallel lines   These are named for
anticipation, for a level of the personal flickering
as clouds trail off   a neighborhood's borders undone by murky air

ALLEGED ORIGINAL

Absence inspired a wish to be unknown
as the occasion shifted with a suspect preference
for moving away from the current into the imagined
luxurious sea, a little bow to the recycling plant.

By some weather? Beyond this one there's a life
and pink sand empty of sharp objects and dead things, demonstrating
variety of species with some sort of metaphor

moments of questioning whether a story will emerge
or leave the pristine for some other assignation. This memory of *garden*
pretends to be nothing else, nothing but an idea
made solid through transplant. Venues grown elsewhere
help form a long bridge crowded with cars all intent on one another
and devotion, move slowly through it until we are prepared

in the awkward stillness. Portraiture in bright sun
is blissful until it meets a central construction of pond and footpath,
water in the form of making air visible. That which we think
occurs only to the graceful is manifested beyond. Purposes elude. Silences

do not. The daring of the shorn, two of the same creature
split by cultivated plants can provide no evidence
in body or other, earlier imitation. Though *disembodied* may feel like
a familiar passage it must be observed that singing does echo
both from one mythology of a large rumbling storm and from
a morning opening into a crowded room. So quiet I could hear my ears ring.

But here among collisions there is not enough preparation
for summer violence, water waiting to spread the streets
and dry trunks swirling into a forest around us. Beneath the changing sky

considering whether happiness is reminiscent of a heavy axe
waiting for use behind a sheet of glass, there are ways
in which a town may be killed off. If we wanted to snake along
this would be doing it. Rows of buttons and ties, of backyards merging.

Around the mobile scenery a system of activity could be
a precedent overturning itself or could be a box containing emergency
                                                                tools
suddenly unsealed, leaving us idle among feverish abandoned rakes
and clippers. What nonsense is amid the senses? Some impersonal
coat of arms was once a marshland, now is a refusal not only to read

but to clean anything made of wood or conduct electricity, exuberant
                                                                enough
to distract the inadvertent phone call from the size of the room
its open windows and the long flat morning visible through them.

OCCASIONAL MOVEMENT

Light assembles then removes itself
in veneration, mannered, care
so taken redundant in name:
be thine forever is a conundrum
underlying attempts to structure boundary

As if ripened in one paper bag
we glow gradually, surface
from urges to take and donate
into a reconstruction of what seems
to have occurred: an opportunity
arising   Pained steps
encircled shadows and persons
yet made space for others

the bright glare of instructions
flung against the time of day and
the daunted, driven from one site
to the original abode
as if part of a sequence torn from
and reattached to narrative

I am longing for structure
for your recounting to illuminate mine
Attempts at description linger
alongside heaps of snow
and rules clouded by
directionless cries recalled
Some lines cut across, depict
while others provide a surface
for circuitous behavior

procedure so involved
that the observation of beauty
cannot take place   Casual hills,
some casual climbing of them,
articulate what might be detected
in the dense undergrowth
padding broken gates
and the language
that accompanies their breaking

A visit was made   We must have arrived
or received, passed beverages from
a makeshift sideboard to
expectant hands, allowed
the fitting of conversation
into places held for dark query

This reply owes its existence to a room
paneled in glass and flowers, to activity
repeated and framed
by luminous color

as if desire
or some mirrored event
were encircled by hands
gesturing concern and the cavalier

in a balance which births *exit*
in the brief interlude
between intent and attainment
Their steady flashes freeze
into clues, carefully drawn
pools singling tap from tap
or metals correlating to sheens
encompassing other substance

FLOAT AND LAND

Excuses repeated thrice daily cease to be identified as such
become philosophy that may float in time, take on traits of a doctrine
                                                                followed
simply for how it is written down   Hand and font

help themselves beneath a row of figures admitting nothing
despite similes ready to encompass the smoke
absented when heads complete the motion of turning, a way
in which to enter a room with hooks and no curtains

Light opens to words provided by the atmosphere, strung by conversation
in an unfettered space that could have walls   could eat everything
if made into meals   Plains beneath begin to prepare
for something to land as we speak from across the street

reminding that silences fill themselves with whatever is available
The smog blended with each sound   twisted
posture made when weight borne is not balanced across the back

Lee Ann Brown

MENAGE A DEUX

a mix of the world, here
of all the works in
          our possible realms
a foretelling   then

a worry,   you say don't
the world has its wears
          and its surprises
both sublime and nasty
I feel a strange peace
          in your arms

from which action
          could happen
          seasonal

Think of how you
          felt as a human
ten years ago
   Who was around you?
   What did you think important?
Here's to that rough
architectural magic, that strange
     presence, exhausted,
then tumultuous, on fire,
     never predicted, yet
eating breakfast slowly
going to work, breathing
off the ferry a little cat
runs across the approaching
dock in the warm breeze
as we bump into the new pilings
I remember my grandmother's

                    White Ford Galaxy
                            covered
                              with
                          loads of pink
                            petals like wet
                                Kleenex
                                  damp
                                   heavy
                                    damp
                    I have a darkness
                    I'm afraid to divulge
                    Name it, bring it into the
                        light —will you still love me?

                    I want so much to open
                    that I'm afraid I might crack
                        —afraid I might freeze

                    ## MAY VISITATION

                    Again at the foot of our first bed
                    Now dark blood-purple tulips
                        have thrust up strong
                    near Star of Bethlehem
                    Red Columbine
                    and all around
                            purple iris
                    wish you were here
                    fragrant & dark
                    all the leaves bursting
                    willow & your wisteria
                    rose leaves mint to list
                    the flowers isn't it
                    enough?

MY EPITHALAMION

a bird sound at the end of every sentence
the period dissolves and becomes a curve of notes

from *lake of souls (reading notes*
— Robin Blaser

on the morning of my would be wedding
I wake up and turn again to poetry
halfway across the continental drift
towards a blazing island
I open the Holy Forest
to middle epithalamion
and later tell Robin the story
of how maybe now
I am married to poetry
and he says But don't let *him* go
and I don't for a little while longer
but now everything is changed and not
so bad as I bed down with poetry and myself
whom I each love intwined real love and would welcome another

THE CURRENT SCENE

I like to see
your eyes
up close

You fill my field
of vision
with a vastness
I like

Velocity stops —
Revs its
Rapid eye transit

its
Car Interior — NIGHT

THE CURRENT SCENE CONTINUED
WHICH I LOVE TO SEE

The World's not safe for Poetry
We must Cordon off the Zones

For even relaxed, sprawling Spring
    so akin to me
Gasped for breath
    to watch film's poetry

Unwind beside me, you
I too love to see

On the bed or in
montage flicker

red velvet arm rest

When you take off
your daily mediating lenses

(which I also love to see
you operating in)
or reflecting
movie flicker

I wonder
who wrote
"potent as were your kisses, enter here"?

not Melpomene
who's skewered
or better
yet
dispersed

OPEN SEZ ME (T&G)

Rabbet is a groove or cut made in the edge
of a board in such a way (thrust back) that a
'nother piece may be fit into it to form a joint.

Wet edge of a rabbetted board, otherwise
engaged to the other,
set down your paying work
& tongue & groove
me again, an autonomous
arbitrix of institutional
negligeé, lost yet again in the dictionary.

PROCRASTINATION SONNET

Be my lesbian cover band while I
again rest and negotiate the ever so scarlet
sparse dream notations as the year
turns red or orange not yet to mark
the students' papers that way since
it's like they did something irreparable

Sheer exhaustion from what?
Maybe I should learn to write
about unpleasant daily world
more or else I'll have nothing
to say

CATULLUS COUCH
To Bill

Good advice: "Start Over"
Today I am Catullus
fitful on my couch

Yearning for a playmate
to "write erotic playthings"
with
back & forth
as we promised . . .

Never missing dinner
Waking from Southern Living

Cows chiastically
low and moan
non-chiastically arranged

O how lucky a poet is
who has only to feed her
self a suggestion or two

and later find it spilled
recumbant
into poems small enough
to carry
anywhere

Falling asleep with the small
green anthology in hand
I read through day-closed lids
illumined

Change this, Lesbia,
(meaning the verses)

Even then our love
remains.

Mary Burger

from THIN STRAW THAT I SUCK LIFE THROUGH

episode 4

a snarled mess. I left you again and again

see blue in the candle flame you'd always thought was orange

mistaken to think the conversation you wanted then can happen now,

relearning life without a favorite limb
I am the same person minus my right leg

talk about which ones of us
are insane
and I can't remember why
I like any of my friends

with the added dimension of age
you can see your own dementia

steal the cross from off the church. create your own religion

the last part of him that could still be called handsome
lightly muscled arms
marred by a few tattoos
stoned all the time but not even that with any conviction

the shock of vacuity after passion

now I'm practicing

dead ringer
        the hollow of a target
    in the middle is a hole

the way one thing in a universe is close to anything else
if "part of" means togethcr
        we are close

            it's never enough to kill yourself

turn your warty, drooling face to me and smile

                            how your body broke
                                at the end of sex's reach
                                I was glad, insistently,
                            to reach the end of you
                    where sex left off,

what was there where something should have been

                    I used to grab your cock like,
                    "this is mine now,"
                    your fingers thick enough to spread my cunt,
            "take this — I don't want it anymore"

                        where your body breaks
                you leave
                we are different

                    ———

episode 5

> tonight I'm crawling into everybody's bed
> and I thank god I am not the Sun King

> screaming through the eucalyptus
> the evaporation of ego is a comfort
> this is not about us

> nobody in the world
> is having exactly this experience

I'm talking
but not to you
      finishing my sentence
as you walk away
      my timing never matched anyone's

> epiphany is a word shaped like aladdin's lamp
> where every wish is the third and final one
>   what would you ask for
> if you knew it would never end?

> all day people have apologized
> for not giving me what I don't want

> thin straw
>   through you I figure out
>   what to watch for
>   (and)
>   what to watch out for

in people

>   dry; not
>   wasted

HOLE *from* BOY

This time when I say dig a hole
I mean move a few shovels full of earth
to make a raw gash with the grass cut away
and the stones streaked white
where the blade cuts them.
This time you come to my side of the hill,
a camp fire burns just as warmly here,
the pond holds light long after the trees
give it up, black trunks etch the fading band of silver,
we run fingers over the ragged bark
catch rough edges, this is sleep
to lean into this solid tree,
our palms and our cheeks stinging.

from MY RECENT DISGUST
WITH THE ACT OF THINKING*

1

A Very Deliberate Impulse on My Part to Foreground
That Intellectuality in a Writing Which Does Not Try
to Shed Its Reflectiveness

The sensibility of Kerouac is that of a refugee or would-be refugee from
the white center who is seeking some alternative to himself, a self he sees
as too intellectual — while in black music he sees a model of spontaneity
and of gut feeling that is exactly what I have been saying is the problem:
an oversimplified "understanding" of what the music is about and where
it's coming from. With Kerouac, I can say I identify him with a white
center. You know, in language we inherit the voices of the dead.

---

*Portions of the text are drawn from Nathaniel Mackey's interview in
Postmodem Poetry: The Talisman Interviews, ed. Edward Foster (Talisman House,
1995).

Entertainment on the way. War is the best time for women. Journal of incidents. Can I get you anything.

———

8

Should There Be Gay and Lesbian Intellectuals?

This is the sort of thing we have had to put up with in my sector of professional discourse. This, I believe, is why the critique of the individual in constructionism — anti-essentialism — is misplaced.

Does Myles speak as herself in the poem? Lots of us are having a bad time at the moment — worse than many of my generation expected. How does Myles' poem reflect the life of John Milton?

———

47

no

                 once

    there was a   subject who   was

            not perfect

    not
    per

    per

               we watched   him   suffer

" "

       it was " " our   ~~sin~~

> *not perfect*   was   ours   *not perfect*
> made us   feel   at   home *not*
> *perfect made us*   all   belong

48

She said, poetry is a marriage, prose is an unfaithful lover.

She said, the phone is not for you   not   for you   Hello?

   In my novel, you

always called

Will you accept —

"Hi

      that's about it

                            clothes
                         off

     "thank

             you no   problem

   no   just
                    back

   is it the   attempt to start or   stop

          that's   harder

that's *what is the meaning of this*
whats this all about

what   the

pilot's last word

NO

no

no

55

It's fairly easy to make something no one will like.

I don't have a fixed sense of self. I find it easy to move from one identity
to another.

You tell *me*.

They said his work was about "nothing."
I knew it was about "me" and "you."

It's fairly easy to do something no one will remember.

If "disgust" and skepticism could be said to be the same thing.

58

I'm not perfect said there would never be another one like me.

"Pisces, poet, and pierced, that's
just about perfect."

I fall back on discursive language because it's comforting to feel my brain function independently of the rest of me. You think thoughts are "invulnerable"? You think thoughts are invulnerable.

If I didn't have a body I would think so too.

I can do everything myself except what only you can do. And I can't do (it) without you.

I think thoughts
vibrating at the same frequency as "you."

How someone so dumb can cause so much.

———

59

Can I tell the truth?
He has a nice dick. He likes to rub it around on things. On me, sometimes.

Brenda Coultas

EAT

Here is my neck. Here is his leg. His leg swollen like a river. Look at his great truck. Look at his wide body full on the bed. Father's father is a headstone of fathers and mothers.
Here a rock. Here a pebble.
A penny
A limestone
A granite
Here a plate of minerals.

Here a gold tooth.
Here a basalt.
Here a salt block and cow tongue.

Here you be there I be buried here and there.

In Lillydale, flows a milk stream of tears. A fine broth of tears and salt (father's father you have made a fine soup here, you've made me a kettle of fish I can't refuse). Your fish is delicious fine bones and firm white.

Your fish I ate into a shape, I ate your fish into a comb. I stroke my hair now. I groom myself with oil. I rake my hair in place. l ate your fish into a boat. I sail away now. I think I'm in the belly of a whale, I'm in a cave, I think I'm a caveperson I think I'm drawing on walls. All of my writing is being written by another.

(i'm in your (a) river. I'm in your (a) mad ocean.)

Deafness, here.
Please work for the night is coming.

Here is my neck, I'm putting it away now (in trunk). I'm putting it away now.

A fine broth of salt wears away the stone. Your statue is fading away. Your fine face falls.

His stone wore away into a lump of coal.

The lambs on the child's stone are gone now dissolved by tears. They walked away of their own accord. I opened the gate. First they grazed as always not realizing that a hole had opened up. They followed the richest grass, it led them out.

I tempered them one by one.

Look at my neck of rare construction, it was broke into. I said yes, it's new again, the doctor made it new again. A construct of turkey bones. A construct of a kite: balsa wood and moleskin,
I'm flying now, Every time the wind picks up I'm flying again. Mother I'm flying now.

recite long string of names here.*(list of family names and random titles)*

The little blue room was pink.

The room changed from pink to blue.

I'm eating you into a shape. I've eaten you into an animal cracker. I'm eating off the rough edges. I'm making shape, I making a smooth shape, I'm evening out the edges now. I'm planning the surface. I'm eating you into a smooth round coin.

Father, please be still!

MY LIFE AND MY DEATH

The killing spree occurs because postal workers are required by law to make bad fashion statements. The black socks with shorts. Who can blame them? Why not the nice brown of the UPS persons or the pleasant khaki of zoo personnel.

In *How to Avoid Killing Sprees by Postal Employees*, the author cites the color blue as the causation factor a catalyst or trigger finger. The blue uniforms (particularly in that tone) repress aggression like a tea kettle without a vent. All that repression is restrained withfn the chest, groin and thighs; is air not circulated, is skin not breathing is blue as a vein over and under the skin running through the body caged and contained pushing at the walls to find the weak spot to allow release to break in the dam become a flood become waves crashing, a wall of red and blue rushing and then still. This could all be solved by painting the post offices vulva pink.

AN INSTALLATION PIECE

God is in the woods hiding his face.
The god of the woods and of the rest stops and culverts and drainage ditches is in the trees. He is painting his face(you will not recognize him. You cannot forward any mail to him He is living in Oklahoma.) He is not an american god so you cannot send him money.

DIORAMA

An army of Wal-Mart shoppers in flag motif sweat shirts block the aisle. This is a year of flag displacement.

Dear Diorama,
I'm swimming in a pool of milk becoming butter as we speak.

Dearest Diorama,
I have a dream complete with dirt and sage. It's a texas of the mind. Life-sized. It's all in my head: a whole landscape made up crushed and turned

to powder. It's a new filmstrip of the west: a bullet of multiple calibers. It's a prickly pear and a sagebrush. A lonesome toothbrush under the pines. I have a waco of the mind. I'm an army of jonestown myself. It's in my pants you know all of it is in my trousers. All of jonestowns is at my lips. I have a little vacation villa set on the edge of the jungle. All of my weapons are secreted there!

We passed the bullets around each taking a bite. The steel between teeth the chips fell. Empty shell Where you from? No answer. Just a hollow core. A bullet with open mouth, a toothless bullet speaking at the public.

Please be my secret agent.
My A & F & T agent.
My F & B & I informant.
My C & I & A covert operator
please be my public servant
my most private pubic serpent.

I have a box of childs of all shapes and sizes for sale. Some in wheelchairs or still nursing. Some to go or to stay. *Do you want to eat them here?*

The children ride in large beetle-shaped carts with faces painted on the front. They ride in a circle around a large toadstool. As for myself I ride a cart pulled by dogs. It's a good cart with fine strong dogs straining against the leather. A bark here and a bark there. Up up and over the hills and through the midway we go. We are very unusual and good at being who we are but no one will pay to see me.
One day I was out walking and came upon a small container of Janet Reno. She wears a nurse's cape and white starched hat. She wears enough white to pass for Elizabeth Dole. Janet is living in a box. She's in the shape of a tv. All the world in on my tv. World, get off my tv. World are you listening? World get off my tv. Well, if you won't get off then please change the channel.

I need a dream to give me some peace. If I had money I'd have some peace. I had 400 dollars once and it gave me some peace. If I had 450 dollars I'd really be peaceful, please give!

I was swimming in a pool of milk becoming butter when they approached.
They offer 2 childs per milk. I was very busy making the right sort of
smooth stroke necessary. I said some one give the childs milk. Someone
come get them please please give these childs a home. The branch
davidians offered 2 meats with toast. Do I want 1 egg or 2?
I'm in a shape of texas. I'm in a shape of America

come and get me.

THE THREE MEN

These three men are saluting America. They love what they do and they
have a good time. They could enjoy themselves anywhere and anyplace
especially if they were being told what to do. If they were in a war they
would enjoy themselves more than winning at bowling and more than
winning at gambling. It would be better to be told to wear camouflage
than to drink free whiskeys all night in a tavern. In the tavern there are
bags of chips behind the bar, but they would rather be fighting than eating
bags of chips. There is a radio on the shelf of the bar. They prefer to arm
wrestle rather than listen to radio. They would like to be told what the
mission is and be given all they need to carry it out. They need direction
from superiors and it's good to be bossed. They would much rather be
bossed than enjoy themselves. Well, actually they'd rather be being killed.

BY THE RUINS

Desperate beverage centers
Your cardboard women are the hearts
Of sadness in fiction!

Angry children admire your rows of bright soda
And lost husbands Whitmanize to the rows of snacks!
I like very much your nature photography

And the total calm with which people return cans
To you, shady employers!
You are not liquor stores.

One cannot get boxes from you.
There is only routine mystery here,
Nothing like a revival

Or a ride in a speedboat.
A speedboat tied to a ruined dock,
That is a mysterious thing!

DYING TO

My old love ripped off of me like an apple
I am dying to see you
To carry you like an age into wood
On my bed like a pyramid on the roof
Rain off the bridge
Searching with a bell
For the remains of the flower whose stalk was found broken
I am dying to crush you
The meteors deliver black notes
Locked like purple weeds

I am without you in a thicket
In the ditch rusted half away
Furiously
I think of you and cough
And what is velvet
A goal of houses
Out with the burning nets and the white mud
Bashing in the floor with light
I write and drop my hand
You find it unintelligible the hand
Blown open by the harbor

THE LOAN

If after one minute you have not given me my floating tea car
I will charge you two oratorios
And every twenty minutes
You must double your style
In an hour eight milltowns
In turn I must agree to maintain the cathedral until such time
As foxes steal gold mice from summer's sling
But if a misfortunate typist
Should scale the dumpster
And pluck the third volume like a birthday harbor out,
Then the stormcloud must yield a key to the ramps;
But one key must remain
Lost in the bushes with the vandalized cravats,
Regretting such has-marks
As strolling permits in watertime,
Running sideways through the blizzard
For the sake of the face.

A LITTLE GOLD BOOK

Up off the ground to the left
Throwing the sun changing its name
Down seventh past tenth past Bleecker
Cars sock at the mouth
Some breezes on the shining bar of soap
What a day the steam coming into the hall
I'm going back into the sky to where my mother was born
To sing a shaped poem upon the spot
Shapely ticket takers in tagalog shoes
Bracelet to the knob a set of keys
Folded church programs on the floor the nib of afternoon
And when I get up blood pinching the gold bandages
The air conditioner works and works
The big old bed like a book as big as a room
Believe me my face on my hand
Fragile sky in the ugly city you see on tv
Turns to gold on the terrible street
The turquoise of dawn is painted on the cornice
I want to run behind the barrier
Of a radio and buy you shoes
The water in white marigolds gauze on your foot
Poor room seen in a bowl beautiful as a school in July
At six p.m. now going underground
She takes off her shoes and puts on sneakers
In the morning come pick up the 8-ball
Christmas barreling through fenders
Of snow black as a cab and in sunglasses I can be alone again
The magazines in the coffee shop are rubber-stamped
Jack-o-lanterns on fire escapes
One hand on the handlebars one hand holding up the guitar
Girl on the corner brought by the octave
Get out and dance on the cracks dirty night feet
Time waving snakes go faster!
The baby in the driveway is hungry
Red spiders give me the first note of a storm
Suddenly the baby sits up

An ice cream truck plying the air
Dont tell me that's the way the blood in the cloth is I know
On the road again the steering wheel my sunburn is healed
Come with me to the city hall foreign dancers on the book of doom
Soft as the harbor the planes scrambled
Falling from your fingers back to the water
The walls put all those strong gold penpoints on the back of my head
I'd have called you north star but I needed to lie down in gold boats
Wrote poems bought with gold for any flower to climb
But I never saw the seashell come up through the floor
Like the noise of a cloud in the intersection
And the light bending through the ceiling with your cat
And the rope rubbing your eye the street door like a hand in your hair
There go the riverbanks again sensitive and false
Careful with that wishbone
All that fever of being caught
That's just the love of the world without you to listen
Virtually all music dreams of you
It's going so fast I have to go to the museum
The ice cream barking all night the piano running past
Please write down the black spark glasses flying
Breathing brick on brick with fires
From within oh dear the trial's begun you're likely to lose
Complaining sunlight
Dying as we do the islands have mercy for suicides a-lisping
Of past fatigue and what judo tragic as a devil in mac
Rain on the roads of the recent past
What did I lose? Tiptoes to flood! And you? More than a dollar
But sweet and easy pants come off
But not smoke on the fold the biblical violin magnums
Cleaned with gold clatter wardens distraught sieve lets rabbits
Age into their veins pink buttons and fifty cigars
So much changed like a rose alone!
The sun of life is missing!
And light a match to start the day
Expecting gray fire of little flowers to sweat and shine
Like perennial tattoos the shout of villains
Snuggling and slipping to move papers

The difference staring down bathers in the morning
Fuck against a wall that stays
To be washed to the bone glitter hello the seam
Is broken from smiling or nail it all lovely as a feather
That couldn't get lost not even in my heart
You can see dream hair on surgery as voice
Lessons roar forward the scream of the news
You cry the sun alcohol busting asks
Hold my hand the summer separating rain from the viola
And Trafalgars from tetragrammata in the morning
Running in the dirt the home of the poem little zinnias
Tuned just above the bosses and helicopters the cinema christs
And why not explode for them at night a fist of pennies
They own guitars and screwdrivers the spine and the bubble
Down streets built of marble and canvas wiving new pasts
Of future late afternoons in August crayon'd by weddings
Asking the number of rooms brightly stocking
Luscious and cold nerves as pilgrims to loathsome stone
Of the next footstep terrible gold lost on me
The basketball under the trees
Newspaper gone crazy on a park bench the long park walk
Asleep I wadded a stop sign into the trash
That's cannonfire this blank July paper flattens out
And that's a tooth red line a garnet tumbled
Light through leaves on a propellor plane
Sleep in love with ink on thumb
A scarf of a black knot yourself a silver stroll in cork
Under the copper breeze
Maybe that's enough loud telephone chess and mild death maybe enough
Ideal points of sugar in hard damnation enough newspaper of mouth
Maybe winds enough driving at night enough clam shell on the chest
Enough skating on the flood floating tulip enough marking the
Lacrosse abominations falling colored air like an arm enough
Where the flames crashed overhead good and bad and hazelnut paradox
Damaged melody of blizzard canal decades and elements menstruating
Me and you not physical or temporary horns in the sun sailing
Chains of grease biplanes novels nature lullabyes bars
Enough just enough adorable come and go keys enemies and clothes

Enough sun and moon eating paper almond storms elsewhere rolling
On a bruise piercing traffic silent churches blazing
Black and red enough ranting to power and keeping quiet until you
Die enough once again and enough no more
It's funny to still get nervous
Across this great red land to be a pattern
I'll be gold and I'll pour water down the mountain
I can see all the kingdoms from this hill
Filled with storms fragile in the distance
Bitter bleach and knotty pine mosquito kingdoms
The palace of drums beating horoscopes
I hear but cannot see the courtiers crouching
Their songs are extra to voluptuousness
Their endless crazy surrender brings the world its fire
The cool land of diagrams of evening and its starry forelock
Its first song pointing to justice
Its second song "Breathe radiant halo of dark rehearsal
"The game preached by sun on a watch
"By force and old water your pages in the daisies
"Do you know what you love?
"Close your eyes
"Then open them down the wall to the black river
"There was the wind and there were trees
"A bracelet lighting the party
"There were people passing by."
That day began with the fall of the water and the light from the sky
Even there the water alone is comforting
When bitter gold is there.

ZAPRUDER

Day off in dark suit & hat,
looking through the view finder
of a new eight-millimeter Bell & Howell camera,
paying no mind the open windows, the seizure.
Just how more than half the targets on the grassy knoll
are potential customers, models, women,
how accident & aim could fit them all,
including the car, into frame. It was the 60's
so before the volume of the motorcade
turned north up Houston then down on Elm,
they passed the camera between them like a joint,
a silent investment. His secretary stood next to him,
confident that their film would change lives,
that what the women wore to greet The President
would influence their sewing machines & needles.
Clicking the power on added something
above & below human to autumn. Now comes history,
that moment when everything begins to wave:
arms, flags, lens, minutes, seconds, silence,
dressmaker, souvenir, evidence.

SPELLBOUND
The Brattle Theatre
Cambridge, Massachusetts

The balcony's filled
with couples wondering
if and how long the hypnosis
will last? Psychotherapy & light
versus darkness, an underground railroad
of hope. Escape,

is that what we're here for?
Eyes glued to the screen have no better
sense of which star to follow
than the blind heart. Peck & Bergman kiss
and doors open that we are not
allowed to see close. Emptying,

an orgy of voyeurs strains
itself through a glass of milk,
a third & thicker lens. Interpretation
of what? The screen goes white,
a cow's stomach turned inside out.
I'd hate to think of slaughter,

lovers at the mercy
of an omniscient somnambulist,
that the brain is a Hollywood filmmaker
crazy with cameras. Odd isn't it,
how if we wore eyes & ears on our chests
we'd have more respect for the heart.

SLOW FADE TO BLACK
for Thomas Cripps

Like a clothesline of whites
colored hands couldn't reach,
a thousand souls crossed
promised air and the screen glowed
like something we were supposed
to respect & fear. Daylight
& Sunday were outside,
waiting to segregate darkness
with prejudices of their own.
A silhouette behind a flashlight
led us down an aisle
into The Shadow World,
rows & rows of runaways

awaiting emancipation.
Theatre, belly, cave,
ate what got in.
We half dreamt weightlessness,
salvation, freedom, escape.
A resurrection of arms
we wished were wings
reached in & out of greasy buckets
picking something the precise
color & weight of cotton.
Just above heads,
Pam Grier & Richard Roundtree
dodged bullets
and survived falls from as high
as heaven—miracles
not worth building
dreams on. And like the ampersand
between eyes & ears,
the soundtrack strung
together images the way
popcorn butter & soda syrup
held us to earth.

PARLIAMENT/FUNKADELIC
HOUSTON SUMMIT (1976)

Notice! Stop! Help Save the Youth of America!
Don't Buy NEGRO RECORDS. The screaming,
idiotic words, and savage music of these records
are undermining the morals of our white youth
in America. Call the advertisers of the radio stations
that play this type of music and complain to them!
Don't let your children buy, or listen to these
Negro records.
          —from a poster reproduced
          in front of the Parliament Tour book

The eye
Atop the
Pyramid

Means

Peek-
a-boo,

Means

We've been
Watching
You,

On guard,

Defend
Yourself,

Means

We shall
Overcome,

Means

You go
Tell it,

We've
Already
Been to
The moun-
taintop,

No need
To reinvent

The hump,

Means

We paid
For the fly-
ing saucers,
Extra-
terrestrials
& maggots

Our damn
God selves,

Not an
Album cover
Penny from
Casablanca,

Not a fold-
ed dollar
Bill from
Westbound,

Means

Pay attention,

Means

IN FUNK
WE TRUST
NO ONE

Except

THE ONE.

SIR NOSE D'VOIDOFFUNK

[1]

That name: D'VoidofFunk.
An expressionistic thing

With do-loops
And threes in it,

Preceded by
A silly-serious

Attempt by
Old Smell-O-Vision

To cop
Some nobility.

[2]

The whole bumpnoxious,
Dark thang stanks
Of jivation

And Electric Spank.
Glory, glory, glory-
hallastoopid.

Then there's his funny
Accent—pitch
Change and delay

Looped through
Feedback, pre-spankic
Self-satisfunktion.

Nose gets harder
As his voice
Gets higher.

Nose won't take
His shoes off,
Dance, swim or sweat.

Nose snores,
A deep snooze,
Snoozation.

[3]

Syndrome tweedle dee dum. Despite
The finger-pointing profile,
False peace signs
And allergic reaction

To light, we brothers
Wanna be down
With Nose. All that!
The girls, the clothes.

Now you know Nose
Knows when to fake it
And when to fake
Faking it.

Waves
Don't mean he's gone
Or that there's going
To be a cover-up,
Very Nixonian.

You can't impeach Nose.
Where's your court-
room, your wig and robe?
You ain't Nose judge.

Somebody scream just to see
The look on our party's
Tromboneless face,
That burial ground

Of samples and clones
Jes grew. A nose
Is a nose is a nose
Is a nose,

so
Wherever the elephants
In his family
Tree untrunk
Is home.

[4]

And that's about the only tail
Mugs can push or pin
On him.

A PSYCHOALPHADISCOBETABIOAQUADOLOOP

All those
    Liquid love affairs,
Blind swimmers
    Trusting rumps.
We wiggled,
    Imagining water.
Wet, where was
    The One?
Nevermind Atlantis
    And the promise
Of moving pictures,
    A lit candle

In the window
  Of our conscious minds.
Those who danced,
  Pretending to swim
Underwater,
  Did so out
Of pure allegiance.
  Some wore snorkels
Made with
  The waistbands
Of funky underwear,
  Others wet suits
With clothes pins
  Clamped to their noses,
Air-tight as
  Black Power handshakes.
Rump-by-rump,
  The strings attached
To our thangs were
  Reeled into The Deep.
Rhythmic as fins,
  Schools of P signs
Flapped and waved
  Like flags.
One nation
  Under a groove.
No one held their breath
  In the flashlit depth.
No one sank.

A BAPTIST BEAT

A mixed congregation: sinners, worshippers,
Hustlers, survivors. All that terrible energy,
Locked in, trying to blend. Such a gathering
Of tribes has little, if any, use for a silk-robed choir.
Members bring their own noise, own souls.
Any Avenue Crew will tell you: nothing comes closer
To salvation than this. Here, there is no talk of judgement,
No fear. Every now & then, an uninformed god
Will walk in, bear witness, mistake Kangol
For halo, all those names for unwanted bodies
Being called home, arms raised to testify, waving
From side to side, fists flying like bullets, bullets
Like fists. Above the snare: two sticks make the sign
Of the cross then break—a divorced crucifix.
The tambourine shakes like a collection plate.
This pastor wants to know who's in the house,
Where we're from, are we tired yet, ready to quit?
We run down front, scream & shout, "Hell no,
We ain't ready to go!" The organ hesitates,
Fills the house with grace, good news, resurrection
& parole, a gospel of chords rising like souls.
Up, up, up up, down, down. Up, up, up up,
Down. Up, up, up up, down, down.
Up, up, up up, down. The cowbell's religious beat,
A prayer angel-ushered through dangerous air.

Ah but who emptied the sand from your shoes
when ye rose up to die?
Sand Israel fetched,
burning sign
I sand, nightingale throat and smashling wing,
longed-for snake dust with
all that fell from Solomonic wisdom mixed,
wormwood bitterness —
Ye fingers
who emptied the sand,
by morning will ye be dust
in shoes to come.

(after the German of Nelly Sachs)

NATURE

(apocologos)

— I hear rumbles —

— that you are going —

— far away —

— O hero, sun —

The clouds, banked

above the car fumes

& the heat of day,

are darker now

6 p.m. & leaving

work, the people

fill the streets

with myth

INSOMNIA

Walking in the rainfinite.
Is it permitted — am I?
— to lag along the fennel track,
episodic?

We, the drenched combines of yore,
depleted,
    gather up the war *repeated* in the clenched kiss
proffered at the door.

He — blemishes — our souls
replenishing the stream
whose icy crystal pours across
a broken length of dream.

CHRIST

The green wingéd lion
prances on a penny jar.
His growls are lost chances
dissonant with Zion.
His tail waves away a star

O to be a girl
and owner of a rounded script
written into remembered nights
haltingly for a pillow
wept upon when I was a boy
and it was summer
trusting

LITTLE WING

The borrowed thing is done with us,
the mangle of its bite
chews the hand around our grasp
and swallows up the night.
Around the bend, toward
yesterday a documented worker
roams. In the hills behind
musicology, beyond the pale
partition, four door sedan
chronolepidopterous

To acknowledge — and more
than that, to emphasize
that language intercedes in all of our
transgressions. The gilt
our tears were worth
in gothic painting

Tears — are our
premise. I knew
a doctor once. She
held me in her arms.
Was not a doctor
then, was armymen
not patient when
we're — harmed —

THE SOUL
IS THIS LIBERAL FALLING AWAY

breathe and disnight, we'll salvage
all that comes by name. Exit
the light she limps
    along
though declarants of never command me
and nothing defend me
save shame

Stung, to please

    the petals of a stem

rapacious scent

I stammer thee along

Wherefore — a flower fades
    and honey turns to stone.
My torn undershirt   my boy
heart wrecked in the night   like a car.

Said the poet, to his poet, you — allot — me

more than I — blighted — ever let grow through,

thresholds to cross in stutter

ever I you

PASSIVE FIRE

held the broken refuge of event
to itself, a war you didn't
want, didn't start
but are

with the jawbone of increase
rush to ocean
where the dark inside of air
interrupts

there is a flower I
can't explain in how
much, over, cast rain

to listen through the roof's
door to the circus music
among the deadly layers

sharp light

curve of Earth

a flying bird in uncreated darkness
liking the fury of it help
all snow and brief bewilderment
of sound, souls in a room

her shadow has taken it back

THE BRIDGE

the river ages the submerged tree
posing as a road, interval
of life from window to window
a body covered in wet leaves
a stag jumps into your path
as you carry yourself down the hill
a first thing, eventually
toward the horizon's
interruption, beacon
dissolved in the cruelty of the storm

mysterious births overtake
the floating tribe
as the pain of an island, or salamander
moving in the ivy
not of opposition, but coinciding with it
galaxies separating and flung deep
blue body in danger
to the green of finding
itself replaced
by a mineral subjectivity
from the forge and predicament
of false yellow

blew through the toll plaza
and stopped on the obstructed
bridge by policeman's light, the blasting sound
from the wielding like the wall-eyed
greeting of the ancestor
supposedly to the guy next to me with the
same name, the bridge disappears
in lurid fog and
recognition, water above and below

kelp, foot, basket and jealous
a kind of prospering

rage the ice on the neighbor's pool
and strange garage

burning unconsciously in consuming

blue of space and tear
myself out of the stupid
jacket that drowns
like a false god into the depth
and transparencies of the stage
the same thread of electromagnetic
credulity rich shadow and
excommunication's garden

PARTIALS

the transparent mine turns opaque
and the blurred faces refuse to overlap

do you believe in this distance?

a cord leads through the woods
to the tongue become some other thing

was there something there you wanted
beyond the stream among dry leaves

to interrupt

I keep pouring fire on the bed
keep exiting, but every morning

it's intact

why am I more alive than these ghosts?

in the earth shedding light

male legs to walk across the sand

a shroud of blood in the head uncoils

Minerva

to come to the end of the alphabet and fall

HEADING SOUTH

an unseen bowl has come hidden from the yes

through lame perdition, one kind looking at another
differently, about to become younger, older

must be the excitement of exposing the scam
meeting up with the are we passengers inside it

how far Weehawkeen seems from here

as love in a porcelain storm overturns the tub

wishful thinking, held together by bands of leather

I hope its not
just sequences of a border unhappiness

she reappears on the other side of

again and in and though and carry
oh, internal mosh pit, containing the joy
of brother and sister just before the A uptown comes through

and did you know that thought was dead?
kept for luck, not out of confused frustration

or honest-to-God derangement

I thought you took the elevator to come out some strange other door
Dearest worm —

how deep the West 4th St. station is
how bright the sunlight in your trench

CELL WALK

What train is this / encased in bones
I carry in my head, the plate
withdraws, through colored absences
the flames could care less about

should I buy the camera or the gun?
trying to decide branches through
department stores of dread

as though they were a weed

follows as a brother as fallow
as decomposing forbears who refuse to exist
or pass away

to eat away the sun
is not a question of being mean

the color of rust
is the rent I pay
to lift a crumb with all their strength

drop it
through unseparated air

looking out of thoughts
that temperature interrupted with a friendly voice

beneath the perceptible forms of sound
is a quiet floor

before the choice is made

moving thing, look down
to an animal that can never remain dead

THE SOURCE LOG

the current to create
or series of nested source
or store without

entering others
appears along the window, **turned**
the car around
to an egret standing in the ditch

the system will reel in turn
within each individual
that sound may end desired time

the first step, the context of a wild duration
"zero" as a line of source's window
will never change the color of the hill

"opens" to the "level" of an individual
becoming memory
to locate the desired end of music

from which this figure, **blackened nuns**
push me off the path

absolute time, is stopped
and hold and never will decay

the difficulty of starting
to close the window
indented beneath a name

repeated error first removes
the second reopens, **reaching
into disappearing
light,** the basis of the current
only sound will not change
the necessary running

**cement dividers won't let me reach the water
in tuneless disaffected night**

name split into parts, multiple
it brings to change
a combination of intentions, so the sound
may be exchanged between the possibility of confusion
don't ever stop touching me right now

by key, then "floating," opened
once the transport remains
is matter, unlike commands
the gates to change to in and from or leading
all that is necessary, the small response
moving as desire

TO APPEND THE ACTIVE SHEETS OF YOU

to append the active sheets of you
this only convert is the present
reflection of sky in pools of water
on garbage bags in the street

changes to create, **like hatch
take hands, tiamat liquid,** there's
no last turn

that lost my ritual hounds
and don't you know where there's a broken grid near there?

like tuba, tide hatch, like lamb
tale kinds, toward an older well
a pump that doesn't work

I lived there once, growing smaller and smaller
kept what I stole and lost all that I earned

don't flee from being wacked upside your head
for very raw indeed is the heart uncooked in the fire of your trial

isn't a shadow in place of life
can read the current to find the name is not another
in the opposite of light

oh you would, *you would*
railroad weight heat withered color slight of ladder to their act

late kinds, ire iamb, take hands
taper lamps ire hatch change-up
won't trace along the form of any human face

as if to exist
intractably

falling through the sky
on a mattress
all the way to the color of the grass

Peter Gizzi

DING REPAIR

There are too many skateboards here, too many
waves to negotiate, the graded hills fall
too suddenly into the sea; from here
that bank of fog turns into a blanket of gauze,
never forgetting anxiety — institutions
are a part of nature though needs
are seldom met in a sunny bureaucracy,
shiny country, for the moment sun-bleached.

Imagining another home far from here
not from where we have come but where we imagine,
where vulnerability won't reproduce cruelty.
A home in the act of finding a home in the act of
what will suffice? No place was set
at the table but you are invented to listen
even if silence is a condition of mind
you will never be forgotten here, where to learn
the speech of the place is to earn to speak in this place.

Said: "I could love you if you left me?"
"No! I will love you if you let me."
Things come to them, a tuning fork
pulling focus, facing each other at breakfast.
Outside sea and sky enlarge the chamber piece,
little flowers dot the hills, for they too
are a part of themselves, parts of themselves
scattered — stuck to cars and windshields.

A hummingbird at the scarlet bell works the vine.
Even as adults we hope to witness ordinary spectacle
evolve into meaning, ordinary and rare each time
the ribbon, the wave — all bent.
For if those memos, phone calls, holidays
were to accrue then where would we be?

If a letter were drafted it would read
the people are cheerful, overworked and kind.
Say there is plenty ocean, plenty sun.
Say we are standing on a new shore
that goes to — if not new — different destinations.
Say these destinations trouble us at night.
There's work to do, faces to study.

Some of the news contains lack —
say the small charge from a battery —
in this way a current flows, querulous
even, a lighthouse has its seasons too.
The metaphor is striking
however like a match making the dark
darker, the night larger
the empty into which we move real.

And holding your hands over your head
reflecting a degraded self-portrait
feel the cord of space pass through your palms
the slow progression of years, endless knots and bits
of talk, lumps of sorrow, nettling of tears.
Close your eyes and find the present flattened.

To speak about distance, memory
a voice stumbles, a flame in wind
when dignity is no longer an option
and rain does not confuse
— folding themselves against the night
into night, or just wearing out the day.

Let the record play, let the notes begin
to make a landscape where we meet beneath
the intermittent sky, let the body evolve whole
rising out of the throat and out of the mouth into night.
Pick up an instrument, play, as though a work of art
were a form, C 38, here fill this out, as though we must behave

as we explain the mess we've made, one note
for citizen, soldier, object, history, but there is no other
door to enter and if there were where would you go
after the masterpiece is finished?

Or a man who can't distinguish the sorrow of the violin
from rust of the old country.
The day sallow and dry leans to the left
the trill accentuates the bulbous tops of trees
out over the terrace, everything in its nest
each unlike each along the jagged edge of horizon
the strings of the instrument articulate each spear
of big ferns across the parking lot.

It is a song that carries this day
yields to the shy, lays its bluster down
tucks in the storms, a new tune atonal for the moment
until the small have grown to embody it.
As though the entire armature
were labeled "heavens" reproduced
inside the home we call our heads
— a ship in a bottle.
Hole inside in the shape of a bottle.

Now when you go to your job, your table or your bed
can you remember this place, a piece
of space left behind, it's not hard to imagine.
Think of an empty closet, some childhood there
an odor of cedar, order of secrets repeat
their sequence and the useless treasure of an ending.

A TEXTBOOK OF CHIVALRY

Learning how to give in to hate, or how to take, in love,
won't recuperate joy, or avoiding joy
might become a paradigm easing a pain unwanted to dissipate.
Is the love a syringe or merely a placebo that becomes habit,
full of promise? Keep the score card close, Cheat.
The earth is still tonight, without a breeze to compensate
for the mind's emptiness. Imagination creates a mother
letting you go free amidst the enemy
because unwanted the cravings grow too, laughing
when promise fulfills its tiny shape. Never
is also part of the greater composition, looking away at the toy horizon.
Who will die from happiness, knowing that their ungainly self was loved
and the clumsy heart embraced? Dinner is never dinner this season,
living in a bubble, the I sinks, I decline too
in this construction even and if only even as the putative author
of these lines, this subject. The subject matters,
wrote the good scribes in disbelief. Wrote the poor.
These slums speak to everyone, don't they, though no one is listening
are they, chevalier? are they? The tribulation of water is heavy.
Out here it is an ocean carries this raft towards something,
something unlike rest, or knowledge of where the surf will crash.
The story of the woman who left the man to drown is the same story
that taught him to swim. When you learn to read water
your fluency increases thirty percent the guidebook says.
The surface is moving as the groundlessness that surrounds one
is more immediate and lowly than historically determined crises of self.
I am waiting for my man, my man has a number in it.
Staged and inconsequential. This may be tendentious
but it's hysterical. Though love is never a joke, even if it feels like a joke:
the clown tumbles to stand up and they are made brighter by their
laughter,
give them bread & circus. Oh *book,* you are a strange friend
but a good one, definitively a path opening on all sides,
as all eyes open, and don't merely gape, but dilate and focus
as with the apertures of the heart. Open, to receive, *become,*
to see, and is it only for honesty in letters that the will founders

before it immolates. Who cannot die, continuing to die,
who has become dead, becoming dead, who will never be dying,
as the hard copy corroborates a twin and the emptiness creates a slave
and the wood recorder releases a sweet note ascending
to embrace these actual clouds in an actual landscape
unwittingly there to coax joy out of air?
Where we are is on a street whose bodies linger, sweat pouring
unlike diamonds onto the hot pavement where
cellophane wrappers say 79¢. Days accrue a hollow dispensation
for time served. The job done. Though some folks sit to themselves
speaking, to no one, neck bent, face twisted.
Is thy bread more stale? Outside is not as far as you imagine.
The voice of a child greeting night.
As a wash of cruelty sets out unlike an imagined river
abrading the tin shell of self-reflection, wanting to be seen.
To be permitted to march against the current
to the "higher ideal" of an unnatural self-reliance,
which seemingly one despises or despises oneself, let go.
To not worry about realism for once, to wonder
without becoming dry. If time is more than movement
of a clock's face, who will witness the supporting parts
before they disappear? To buy back the empty lot, to build
a fascinating life so it takes another lifetime to read it,
never to understand why one is here, or why now,
or who or what they shall become, whence written down.

AT EARTH

At this end there was silence, silence without earth,
        and the silence wasn't earth.
It was different at the end without earth.
Nothing was undone by a world; or with world nothing wasn't undone
        that wasn't already undone.
Outside world there wasn't death; as dying isn't the opposite of life.
The silence was part of life; or in living silence was misrepresented.
This earth came into being without a name; without a link, men disappear.
Without words, the word is undone by silence; and becoming multiple,

is without reception.

Becoming without reception, dispossession was taken away,
  but not to those without linkage.

Someone died, being wind, the allegorical aspect of wind, and
  of the fortune of life, without silence, a blind counselor.

The silence is undone by wind, is outside (seeing nothing, nothing
  was seen), empty of speech.

That which is before no one isn't disliked after one: it comes after no one.

An emptiness which can't be provided.

The silence disavowed the word, and laughing whispered, that which wasn't
  anarchy came by the lowest of means.

Everyone is a witness to the blank once in a while, every forgotten father,
  cast off the bench, a ward of the state, who renouncing whom.

LIFE CONTINUES

Life continues while the telephone intersects continuity with another party.
The day will occur with or without your approval, though to get you on
the wire and arrange a meeting is sunny. A forecast of hope has provided
excitement this afternoon. No, a forecast of excitement has provided hope
this afternoon.

       The world happens at your doorstep. There is no method
to decipher this day. The birds and the bees are both moving geometric
patterns. To connect one plain with another horizon. There are doors
everywhere we walk and occasionally stumble upon a carcass, which now
is only a frame – the door is ajar. This place once marked an exit. Today
it is a wall. Where is the magician of openings?

       To question the infinite is
an inarticulate gnarl, better to blur at the humidity of touching. Love, I
stopped by to pitch some woo, we walked to town in Chinese shoes.
There are doors into which we can enter, to move through this room,
indecision and terror. That the light is blinding over there or the darkness
here is without hospitality is beyond my calling, though limbs answer and
bear solace for a space called imaginary time. There is no measure of year
or day let alone now held in these arms. Time kept on a clock whose
hands are beautiful, to say you, here, or there you are, is irrelevant to this
field of stars. The night yields repose of the unknown, for the physical has

no identity, is why we close our eyes when we touch one another, and this *one* is felt upon the flanks of my body's shivering and released at the nape. Only how to resolve this face before me? Facing the horizon of my shoulders.

Bless *you.* The *you* now here in italics, the you of the ways, you of the aquamarine, you with the oasis touch, you of the pandering smile, you with a greasy heart, you lacking denouement, you of heroic conceits, you who forgot, you who did not awake, you who awoke and cannot forget, you of the suicides, you with murdering hands, you of the carbuncle gaze, you who will die, you who will not die, you blush, you blur, you in the figure of a question mark, you are, this *you,* you too and you and you and you.

NEWS AT ELEVEN

The treatment of the missing fare
will not account for absence
equated on the astrolabe of memory.
This in itself some achievement
of unnamed organs of discourse,
like a hippogriff in dreams
on wet lawns of Saturday eve
with Betty and Veronica, such pastel
impossibilities in adolescent moonlight.
Walking the boulevard through the years
you arrive always here about to depart
and going return for the lastings
and stayings of reflexive reveries.
Although time past will become a new
setting in the parlor, recalling
the light of a passing day's impression,
played severely upon the ceiling.
Night meditations of personal
adventure. So let's go back to
that sunlit beach or to rivers
and mountains if you prefer
a device, then one will be fashioned

to employ all the colors of that
faded photograph with what's his name
laughing so intently in the moment.
But it is precisely not that moment
with which you adhere, and tracking
the affect there is another event
with its own colors and agenda,
sounds from which your present gestures
are drawn to try with words, to infuse
a specific feeling, though displacement
follows your every so-called denouement.
So return to the glow of the television
and car horns outside
that startle only for an instant,
though the message is closer to
those sirens, the ones you wake
to in the periphery of sleep.
"One of our submarines is missing
tonight," and to begin here
is a rope looking for an end.
Conclusion may be convenient
if not altogether catastrophic.
This report is inadequate,
no graph to illustrate a fear
escalating beyond, any rational
notion of belief, systems
to produce the intangible
dividend of change, an address
of one state to the next residence.
The house uncommon in its foundation
is set precariously out on a limb
or latest whim to inspire
a feeling of security, an operation
of trompe l'oeil employed at all the seams
to appear invisible.

DEUS EX MACHINA

I guess if we get to be here today
and watch this movie together
it has all been worth these past thirty odd years
it took to get here
on this Tuesday. In this city.
Is why I'm here. To know you.
I will compare knowing and saying
and tell of all such coordinates
that run together to the river replete with its ghosts
in this instance of talk.
But we won't scuttle. Will we?
As it gave the first buoy of its name.
Friendship, so entire, so perfect
you will hardly find the like elsewhere.
Even if the buildings are all in disrepair,
please, don't let that inform us.
It's meant for us, to pass by that dogwood tree
in May as our voices carry into Thursday twilight.
May I keep this promise?
Along with those petals flaunting the new season.
Little pennants of time. Boundary stones
to be collected on the periphery, where I live,
and where I remain, so I'll be here thinking of you.
Don't worry. I'll work hard. Places everyone.

When sunlight accumulates in afternoon.
A box of elderberry lists behind the alcove. . . .
Then description fails the reader and we
are left with only shapes and patterns. Still
a single leaf trembles on the breeze.
Emblematic, a lovely badge, serrated
and at peace with the day that has flowered
beyond the notion of our need.
Where the reader lists. The poet builds a room,
it can be small or grand depending on the tone
as in June her garden is real.

An intricate lace of affection to correspond
when wanting fails. Perhaps a yellowed doily
on your grandmother's nightstand
like a tune, long off, played
on a toy piano. Clink. These lapses
from time to time fill hours and cars
on the highway. A room to include your ramble,
as well as itinerant interlopers visiting
from unforeseen lake districts — with its news
of festival lights and famous contests —
where the song dies down into rotting hulks,
trunks exposed at the sleeve of the shore.
These transitions or seams if you like
inform me. Water and land disguised as matter.
A carcass dressed and open for inspection
revealing nothing but process, lovely and
inescapable from our own play.

I was waiting behind the skene, worn,
ravaged from too many trips to the provinces,
too many performances, too many nights
accosted by the rabble. Some people got a lot a gun.
What makes you different? Show me.
Here's a dime. Call your dead
and find out what they've learned.
Having been too preoccupied with the house
and its metaphors and where
the objects would lead them. Too selfish
to watch out for us. Abandoned,
beautiful and wide-eyed, developing the tools
to maintain the glorious liberties we carry
in our hearts and pockets. Then something
else did come to stand in its place: namely you.
Which is where I'm going tonight,
despite the distance from seam to shadow.
For I am relative to your I, while
this page walks into my side, where
the sun sets. It's a special light this.

When evening takes a sip off the din
of long endurance, becalm, be near me
always — book. So I and I and I we go.
Together under the elms. Won't that be nice?
To watch one by one all the colors
drain out of the sky into our organs.

POEM FOR JOHN WIENERS

I am not a poet
because I live in the actual world
where fear divides light
I have no protection against
the real evils and money
which is the world
where most lives are spent

I am not a poet
because I cannot sing about
lost kingdoms of righteousness
instead I see a woman in a blue parka
crying on the street today
without hope from despair

I am not a poet
for there is nothing I can say
in smart turns to deflect
oncoming blows of every day's
inexistence that creeps into
the contemporary horizon

I am not a poet
but a witness to bear the empty
space that becomes our hearts
if left to loiter or linger
without a life to share

I've seen sorrow on joy street
and heard the blur of the hurdy gurdy
and I too know what evening means
but this is not real — poetry is
and from this have I partaken
as my eyes grow into the evolved dark

Renee Gladman

ARLEM

she said because I was cute I could slide with only five
dollars, the Chinese woman with yams. Because I was
cute: the front row second seat, Latinas named Lillian and
Elisa, White girls I forget, you writing about the traffic
from what is seen to sawed (getting us coloreds in print)
and the poet's hand on my back. This means you she said
pointing to her lips or lips speaking. I could not decide
and for the pains of determination, I didn't want to.

———

a woman began her poem with invitation (she said) we
had used our color to get inside but that was not the point
and I laughed. Or what is usually seen as laughter but
closer to measure. I felt uneasy and thought to empty
myself. She began her poem: we had used our color to get
inside though codes were undoing. And we crowded in.
Still talking about birds.

———

in the dark again the words come as interruption; she
wants to know my zip code. "I have a letter in my name
juxtaposed to your skin color." What was her plan because
we are all so secretive when we're afraid or disgusted.
I took a deep breath, but stopped short with applause
afraid of misunderstanding my tone. Your skin color?

———

on another day (that we're not talking poetry) she was the
reason I came. An introduction, ourselves before the
mirror and her saying that's how we met. Being cosmetic
where we should have been commotion. She let her
guard down and biting relieved me. On that day
everything meant something else: I was cool as black.

———

she (who they thought) was confused by proper nouns
ain't. Or so she would tell the audience: Asia is not one
place nor many places but thoroughly separate so speak of
me in kind. When in my dream the next night she sat up
front with the Filipina organizer I must admit my spit was
hot. This jealousy, she called it, made us one something
you call Asian but that's not right. And surprised by my
own complicity, this all the time being the only black
thing, wrote this.

———

why I avoid the active in her (conceding some aggression
to complement you) doing what the living does. Our
conscious acts of preparing food we put turnips on the
greens side of the place though they yearn for the
heartside and nothing in the middle, cornbread always on
the table — indeterminate and somehow more patient than
the rest. Macaroni, not next to cranberry, but yes sweet
sweet potatoes. And don't forget your dressing, not inside
but in addition to and where will we put all these elbows
and fresh knees.

———

she wanted to hear what I said so she could tell me what I
did so I made fantasies sound like dreams, a metaphor for
this case or that case. I refused to specify. This poetic
ignoring her soft neck while we talk politics disrupts the
closure of thinking. You are never just the period or the
pause, but the mouth turning up or down and my wet
teeth glowing. She called it a shame that I used language
to make us strangers pacing between the social and sexual
"before we resolved ourselves." But how can I show my
face in public without first making it up.

———

"because everything is and is not, I may lose my identity!"
Or as she is saying this (what you call showing the brush
stroke) the eye falls on the hem of her skirt, thighs parted
slightly. Maybe if we move language to its z-est or
atheorize the length of lines, I wouldn't wander. But the
body floats on strange water and at night I make lists of
revolutions. When you said to listen was a revolution
and to touch her hair, you were talking about poetry and
seaweed. That we could take life and disorder it just to
laugh at the residue.

———

as if sweat began with the experience of poetry, I thought
this: by the last line she was on her haunches so as to
always be behind me. A way for us to show our private in
public; we were getting down to it. Language was a
promise and somewhere in there our lines broke. It was
the sweat on their skins, one hovering the other; the taste
of salt between creases.

———

———

having decided on neither extreme because she is always
already in the middle I sat through intermission tapping
my foot to its duration. You ask me why I mourn the
leaving before you have left as if any answer would bring
us closer to the problem of poetry. It is not your actions I
mourn but what I must invent as a result of them.
Solitude has a way of draining my intentions. It rains and
I drool on you.

———

a poet (who is beside herself in drag) is trying not to be so
many things. She mentions over coffee. This naming of
dishes before we dive in, all the pauses of presentation. I
cannot be everywhere at once. She being 'at peace' with
the singular while I is a constant dispersal makes her hard
to recognize. The way a double negative brings us full
circle. To speak of oneself in language we are always
closing our fingers in doors, lamenting the process of one
topic of discussion — our words returning to a single stone.

———

thinking about the speaking subject, if she should go out
or not, or rather this business of identity deferment I
want to use my social constructions to emphasize it.
A woman (who is tired) does not enjoy ambiguity if it is
used by someone younger than she. A possible contact,
she would be one I turned to, except on the occasion
that I am vague. And then on that night I would have
clearly sold out.

———

someone said convention was the avenue to expression,
that is, if you are thrown by your disposition. A confusion,
I think, of one's story with what it takes of history to
hear it. We are not out to be linear but are linear just
the same so I kind of let my beard grow. When suddenly
you occurred to me, subjectivity was a pressure similar
to desire, an indication that one phase had ended. We
were sometimes standing outside for another's attention.

———

the indigestion that made me still while the crowd roared
was not indigestion. But the body knowing before I that
you were a small breathing in flames beside me flipping
through the program. The shift of particular motivation,
I squeeze my thighs tight to keep from sharing it. But
forget to close my mouth. You said as a recollection of
intent that it was not the sound but the posture that drove
you, the insistent opening door.

———

we seem to have slipped into a poetry that is hard to
designate. We say it, though not this, and she expects you
to follow: the straight couple next to me debates the
horrors of sexuality which means sometimes I am not
where I say. But to the matter of your lack of devotion, I
have seen the crack house next door and the woman
dancing all day on the corner. She tells me I walk too
close now.

———

"you realize you have a body the way your bark does."
She is thinking of all the separation of I is this thing and
these others when she remembers his existence, that in
some place there is a point to her receptacle that she can
either touch or ignore. And you can have yours. So
when the man (who uses his name in jest) says nubia to
get a hard on I smile to keep from him these.

———

walking home from the show (you might say) endangers
her sensibilities. He was looking out. The myth of
disappearing at night. It is daunting to up and end the
enjoyment of darkness because we are made to see
ourselves opposed to light. And losing. Is ever losing the
poetics of black. So between the possible and fear of the
possible she wants to be herself and nobody in the
neighborhood.

———

when nobody walks her dog I am afraid barking will call
attention to her shoes, my only extravagance. The way I
dress up so that eyes may land on the sky. Because she
wears her hats like scarves I return to culture with
questions of servitude: who is pleased with me. A
solidarity perhaps with what the past said, but will she
ever shut up. This being the science of absence, I have
come to learn it upon measuring myself to her. We were
in a room being entirely physical yet not speaking.

———
———

how is it we begin by knowing ourselves so little and
others none at all. I cannot say how lonely we are but will
ask you to come inside. She thinks of another difficulty,
something off cuff: the bunion on her right foot, two days
with rain, and saves time to leave quietly. This problem
of the person (she stretches across days until we find
watching walls an inconvenience) the process of
documenting what she has never seen. We have gotten
in beyond our ability to rebel and are motionless.

————

suddenly the motive of perceiving oneself as indigenous to
these parts or somehow followed by the idea of a center
(she has no problem walking up hills) becomes the focal
point of any presentation. As if the moon is more full the
day after, her dialectal imagination, these curly cues that
were not here before. At some moment in our driving we
realize the one way moving forward as we are in our
weakest state. She saves your notes on tomorrow.

————

to be angry for the first time means she has finally found
the edge We sat for hours in the rain. You had arrived
but could not remember your mission so I said: there's
something telling me your mouth is full of bones. And
we were like that, full of and like that for some time.
When again she found the frame our stories had shifted;
you were me and this dangling.

————

because your fear implies that she should loathe the very
thing she is doing, you wear this way. And the body flails
with affection — is it safe here? — such that there is this
distance between us. And the theory of revision continues
for this generation. We spend more time on what we are
saying, nibbling at the thing. You want to evoke signs of
the living she said that's why my repetition.

———

conjuring a scheme to undermine sexist society he
entertains the possibilities of delayed eavesdropping as if
language twice removed would extenuate the
repercussions of saying fuck her and meaning it. I don't
know. To every space retracted we tried to insert her (so
there will be less he's you said) and found ourselves
forcing the circle. That we may now chart the person in
opposition to the themes of his naming, we are thrilled
where we don't have to tell him because he is always
asking. But all of that is being political where I only
meant to impress you.

———

she responded to his question about the delineation of
power between us by saying we are both obviously
aggressive, which implies that the scene my become
violent and we might win. You say I admire the way
events finally lend themselves to clever articulations but
where was the threat when I needed it. So it seems the
past is always with us and to have survived it makes her
gritty. These days (he said) you have a preference for art
that respects your space by offering up its own. And we
are talking in on ourselves.

———

an adjunct to any reality is the writing of such. With that
she intends on being painterly (unmoved by concerns for
unspeakable dimensions) she has come to observe things
carefully. what one might call scientific collapsing. You
once said there was a difference between what something
does and what it originated to be and we would see it once
the thing became public. Which means the presence of
what I cannot define determines what I hear so that you
read doubting me.

———

the movement embedded in anticipated discourse, his
contradicted perspectives. We sat around a table getting
the pain out — the first of any kind, a rough
interrogation, the room splitting it seemed. You said that
every grid had an opening, some counter to the frame and
we were upon dissolving to talk real for the first time.
Thus it is only by our passion for speech that we evade
change and risk one another so as to wipe again the
surface clean

Judith Goldman

proprioceptive commands

I have saved these words for this event

because here at least you see things
as they really are,
not dressed up.

allow me to play a tape-recorded speech, I talked
it over with the photograph of my wife,
are you sure it wasn't you?

there's no crime in disagreeing.

what you need to do
is prevaricate

all following from there

but more than this
you'll wish you did later

I'll never get the chance again

———

once I knew how to
suitably disguise
my ignorance

carrying my own lamp
in its own right,
an overly natural native son.

take me at my word.

I abolished myself as a nuisance,
and maintained myself as an institution.

I took it out in theories;
parody began at home,
but where did home begin?

how pain petrifies the threshold

between predescessor and throwback,
coxswain and dedicatee,
dejecta and relic. I

know now how

they say one content is better than two

a criminality prefabricated,
defenestrated and reabsorbed

a discordant proverb that sings
a world of hereditary quiet.

———

then how comes it, born originals,
we die copies? new
metal at the mint but
grown fat by another's food,
abegging with gold in purse.

asphyxia shows your breeding
testimony generation

even this abstracted,
ears refined and broken
or engrossed, engorged
sated and

duplicate in stricken
pluralagia, a madding crowd
looking after the philosophers,

are they there?
they are there,
true enough,
there they are.

behind the counter,
hired hands

———

asseverated flaneur,
nailed down in tremens

we say our sugar and flour are clean, our
halfcocked ideas reerected

before the charges of the light brigade

I told you
about the dream in which
the landlords are after me

are all seditions unalike?

attend me, attend
my vehicular crimes

the caption read:
        the living dead.

———

would you mind spelling me for a moment?
I am an excellent correspondent
but I fail to see the connection, after all

after all, the order in
which events occur
should not determine their importance:

you went to the bathroom,
washed under your arms,
put on a clean shirt, a black tie, and a dab
of the Spanish scent
you had bought in Madrid
in Nineteen Twenty-Seven.

the part time
played is not

our only opening
onto the world

the person who we are is geography and

nothing connected with discovery

is foreign to us

slough off grief, it divides
you, you
have to say goodbye to
your past life

take shoes from someone who froze in the night

how else does a triumphalist turn tricks?

———

and you
are you quite potempkin married
subtle brute?
I mind me how when I first looked at you,
an isothermic venture halved the battle
to guide the shivering bark to its disembodied
lull.

O, logomemnon, your lemon
is leaking my lesson!

the climate isn't even useless

and in this capital disaster,

my bush was not consumed

I a'
dress you, so to speak
through punctuated equlibrium
palpable,
distinguished, discrete.
if I beg you lay down
your arms to me,

your other arms will fly up

it must forever be ridiculous.

———

still

attend me,
I doff counsel sotto
voce, but sustained

I only mutilate what has already been repressed
I can imitate the angels, too

holy holy holy holy

who journeyed to denver, who died in denver,
                                who came back to denver &
waited in vain, who watched over denver &
                                brooded and loned in denver

o keep the Dog far hence

if we can't get there in time,
then we just won't see ourselves

———

I bemoan the loss of all manpower

as we stand here waiting for the train

we become at home as prisoners

you, Crowd that flows over the bridge
are you conventional or convention itself

the person who we are
approximates the remote

there is no danger, no danger
that becomes you

delusion, if delusion be
admitted, has no certain limitation
but to fall in

preoccupied with
the opulence of occupancy
vocation

that a mind thus wandering in ecstasy
should count the clock,

retard victory

———

you seem distracted.
shall we discuss Gehenna,
exagerration, paranoia?

is shock the issue? shock won't change anything
there are some very good
feelings
that may have bad reasons, don't you know?

my folded fan,
we are transient shepherds
who stow away

afloat the grim
prospect of real property;

on pirate backfires,
we blow breath
between the small
hard teeth of worms

this secret I secrete
how strung,
        how cold
these words could have no meaning
grotesque and insignificant

a vocation of evocation
I miss the mark

excuse me
excuse me
authenticate my fraudulent abridged duress
requite my decrepit invasion
with exhorbitant alarms to quiet
the idiot questioner

rewind the wrecking ball

————

omitting all disturbing accidents,
we are packages of leaking water

to be thick with
depth is shallow, piss in the soup
so as to speak.
the whole earth hidden in an urn
altogether felicitous, complete.
all famous human endeavor
thoroughly identical.

the person who we are
is the ground beneath our feet
to know your enemy,
enter his terrain

follow the nihilismus
you can't follow, farther

finally

————

father, father
orchestrated center

brusque humours and complex ambitions
compel me
to bite your hand.

I lose sight of the preamble,
digest the martial pulp.
the hearth dissembles and grows cold. . .

————

anaesthetic would upset everything
if I rise from the dead, you thought. if I rise
from the dead will I be stuck with these people in straw hats?

you must forgive me, I am a synchretist,
I've drawn ideas from here there everywhere

you see, you don't abandon a concept as you might a dog

since I'm here, why don't you take me
for a dance, you numskull,
hallucinations are also facts
the music's nice and it's a marvellous evening.

having your wits about you, you might
have written me a few lines
by which to measure our shadows.

I myself am as a rusty key that has no lock to fit it

I wrap the gentlemen in my more rawer breath

I use this hammer to chip away

your face, as a song

———

yes

I pries you and you goes out the door, known
for your notoriety;
it's just not anonymous anymore.

but how did it became memorable,
particulars acquitted to our characters,
making our names?

the two words in the language I most respect are Yes and No

but history is more imaginative than I am
it's not the sort of animal you can domesticate

If I rise from the dead, I thought, will I
eat men like air?

I'm on the telephone

hello, this is my father

I'm being disingenuous

this work was to be heard only by the Central Committee of
the Party.

in another ten minutes

I shall begin to laugh

Yuri (Riq) Hospodar

SPIRITUAL

For a prehensile tail! I would recognize the universe
of undesired governments and frogs!

For charm! I would scatter all my debts upon the soil
and bring them up green and feed wet children!

For a legible desire! I would sell cars in Fresno to grandpas
whose brethren run without bowling shoes in broad day!

For a tonsure! I would bellow God through nostrils
which partake of utter forests, whole trees!

For a turquoise mind! I would blow a whole swim team and never
take credit, leave them secure in their spermy secrets!

For sleep! I would relax my glands and the glands
of all others, trials of amazement and dexterity!

For gills! I would take a fresh language, salt it well,
plan its stretch of marketing manuevers!

For evangelism's death! I would coil alone, drop hints,
leave room for spider bites!

For new time zones! I would lock up the keys, border them with
hedges of my one-night-stands!

For love! I would clap my hands from atop all walls,
sing the name of he who dreams me!

For a Norse! My Vikingdom for a Norse!
Oh blond gods, let me smell all rigid things!!!

ONCE UPON A TIME

Once upon a time
Hell was a hot place,
children were seen and heard
and there were things in the forest
that would talk to and eat you.

Once upon a time we were living
what we'd club to death and stuff into poems,
each day a prepubescent greenygold time
with clocks decorations for kitchen walls
and no authority outside the room's domain.

Once upon a time my just-bathed summer night body
watched cheesy TV interrupted by dissent
before the Baby Boom bought their way into the networks
and forced me to watch sitcoms in which they cope with
                                        themselves.

Once upon a time rock and roll was a threat
and not a Time-Life anthology,
giving those before me something to do with their hands
before mine felt the need to stray where they didn't belong
before hormones ran out of the recording studios
and the vacuum was filled by corporate promotion
and though my hands went nowhere new
        they went unaccompanied by an insurgent soundtrack.

Once upon a time '64 the last year of explosion
the Baby Boom ended, me its last word,
but with no virgin syllable, no air left unbreathed,
no ideals left to live instead of pine alter,

nothing to do but watch it scatter before me
like the Challenger: dreams waking themselves up
while I'm just laying down, just watch the greying of America
while I'm still getting hair in necessary spots.

But too something to learn from;
   a guide where maybe youth shouldn't have one,
but there to be worshipped, wrestled with, perhaps
   rejected, like all other things these days
as institution (only) coming into power
   rusted, warped;
one more view to choose from the television set.
Like the '20's, like Romantics, like ancient Greece,
   a documented era to draw from
   (with discrimination) and use:

but I was born there, a bit too late in accelerated times:

once upon a time fantasies lived and I began to:
the last word of the Baby Boom;
while they sell off what they can
I keep what I can,

here to be perhaps a bridge

or at least give it a good
Viking funeral.

THE CLARIFIED MOOSE

I want to bounce;
faster, faster, like the high winds in hurricane trees.
My life (this life) is a coffin of gravity
and I tire of unemployment's mythology.

The sun turns my kitchen (this kitchen)
from its ordinary foggy morning too-bright yellow
to an explosion of mustard, I
am in the condiment container of the Castro
neighborhood, a place once called Eureka Valley —
still so-called on the hetero maps,
like the white man afraid of the Congo turned Zaire,

or the Christians pale at Persia *nee* Iran.
A change in name is a change in power.
Perhaps I will turn into Greta, or Butch.

Some charms work in the lengthening vocabulary
of what I'm willing to try for effect,
to make things happen, make things mine:
clarification, an altered spelling, a new way of saying
the old things' names I'd change.

EGYPTIAN FOREPLAY

Ah, love, let us be glued to each other!

Don't you see what a desert this is,
and that all these monuments built to last
will just last till a time when they make no sense?
The road to hell is paved, boy, paved —
remember that when you're walking the streets
headed for the high priests' temple-a-go-go
where the ever-ready acolytes writhe all at once
and eyes and arms lock yet never meet;
remember that when your eyes start to glaze
from predatory overdrive, and blur from exposure
to building humped on building —

the Moon was a perfect crescent last night,
the rest of her disk a benevolent phantom.
Let us go where the Moon can see us,
and only our eyes risk outshining her.
Let's lay by an oasis, on a Bedouin blanket,
hear her sing through the trees,
and in reply, we will breathe.
Your every touch is a new religion, as old
as life; let our pulses be our rhythm,
not the proffered excesses of a priestly machine.
Take off that silly hat, let me loosen your sandals;

let our feet rest, let our eyes meet,
let our lips and hands go where they may,
where they can;

we will explode in the night into thousands of pieces,
scattered in the sky, gathered by the Moon,
caressed and placed by her back where we lay,
coiled so close that the sand couldn't cleave us,
even if it tried.

DWELLING ON/IN

I twirl the globe
and land my finger
squashing the city
he's in this time

and in that
other-side-of-the-world
night
no one sees
the big shadow
of my consideration.

Moon, I call,
if you're not too busy
making werewolves
and dodging satellites
put on the
old broken mask of Love
just once more
and with a hard
foreign languge
whisper my name
in his ear.

FAILED ODE TO THE DOG
(after meeting the living inspiration
for the film "Dog Day Afternoon")

These topics of sociopathic innocence
are difficult to sing
without sounding trite or wilfully decadent
Some songs are in keys
those unwilling to sing
become unable to hear —
but the rare dog
in a dull human crowd
will hear, and howl,
songs of his own without care
or conception of rules, of laws
that others implicitly accept
and, when attempting to rebel,
can only mimic what few canine tones
reach their ear —
and mimic flatly, faulty,
at that.

And that rainy night next door to the Monster
among the burgers and beer
and the shining brown eyes of the boy to my side,
amid the corrections and addenda
to public versions of his tale,
his family pictures
(all but one wife male
and several cute)
and accounts of improvised weddings
and the bank siege itself,
I too perhaps heard
some untranslatable tones
and I will savor them,
unsingable, invisible as they are,
and wait for the world
that will give such sagas room to grow —

for necessary as it is,
I fear his epic poem is not in me.

How can I quote press clippings
passed round the table,
or the invitations offered
to almost everyone present
without using those three overkilled terms —
"sex", "drugs", "New York City"?
I lack the skills to toss them about
without fearing I'd sound like
an art student thinking
he's a goddamn Bukowski,
or like I'd listened too long
to Velvet Underground records
with a facial expression pretentiously nocturnal —

I'd never captured the energy in those eyes,
that transcendent trickster glee to be alive —
I'd fail attempting to sing such freedom,
to cage it in words.

Such a song isn't taught to us;
we must forget the scales,
to sing in such keys.

I wait for the day I can hear such sounds
and howl along in tones all my own,
because to reject law is human:
to be free of it,
canine.

BEATRICE HAS LEFT THE BUILDING

She had the penthouse apartment in the Hotel Afterlife
and never felt good about it.
Her name, the acclaim wrought on her
by some fellow townsperson, a kid with a crush
she barely even knew,
had somehow gotten her publicity enough
to earn top spot in this place of literary lovers.

The damned guy never even stopped by that much
once he arrived at the hotel too:
kept planning parties in the Poet's Wing,
with Virgil and Homer, a few others he thought equal
heading over there for wise discourse.

She began to wonder if she'd been just an excuse
for this guy to get in good with the poets,
get a free tour of Hell, Purgatory, and Heaven
(three dull places no one in the Afterworld goes to,
but for his entertainment Virgil dragged him around)
and, surprise of surprise, return claiming to find
his friends in Heaven and his enemies in Hell,
and get some revenge by writing all about it.

And then, a few weeks ago,
word spread through the Hotel Afterlife,
accommodations being made for a new arrival,
one better-loved by a lesser-known poet,
and whose impact on the living world
has just begun to be felt.
Rumor reached her of this to-be-honored arrival.

Being Beatrice, after all, she got a peek at his resume
and biographical sketch, and saw his achievements
and a seven years' love shared and then cut short.
Heck, the other guy's poems about him
weren't half-bad. And at least he'd shared time
with who he was talking about.

Beatrice was respected as a classy person;
when she came to the Hotel Afterlife's manager
and requested a Change of rooms,
no reasons were asked; a fine suite was found
between A.H.H. and Pushkin's unknown asterisked love.

And when she went to the garden and gathered roses,
knowing his love would want him welcomed thus,
walked down the tree-lined road to the gates,
and sat, in vigil, awaiting his arrival,
the grounds-keepers gratefully delivered messages for her.

The penthouse was to be just slightly transformed:
Galileo and Copernicus (her dear dinner friends)
were to oversee addition of a private observatory,
the best telescopes and such equipment to be found
installed in time for his moving in.

A grand party was planned:
the astronomers mentioned above, of course;
Isaac Asimov, Konstantin Tsiolkovsky, Gerard K. O'Neill
would all be there, while the finest chefs ever to decease
cooked up a meal no guest could resist.

And later Leo Ford and Joey Stefano
with some other dead gay porn stars
would show up to play, in any manner he pleased,
when the science talk wore thin
and the evening grew late.

And as wave after wave of all the guests
Beatrice invited would say their good-nights,
and Todd B. Hawley was left to stay his first night
in the penthouse apartment of the Hotel Afterlife,
on a table with roses she had picked in my name
he would find a glass of wine, with instructions from Beatrice
on a trick of which she'd heard:

on how to enter dreams, and while one's love sleeps
the sleep of the living, take the glass to his lips,
whisper his name — let him hear your voice, even if just in dream —
soothe his pain with the Afterlife's wine,
say you're having a great time, everything's fine,
and let him know you'll be waiting when it's his turn to arrive.

from *SEA LYRICS*

I am a partially submerged boat on the waterfront of
Jack London Square on a Sunday morning buying
jam. I am flesh-colored and pale, in an indian head
dress cracking chestnuts and eating roots, in the
fissure between the bus lines, with the smell of burnt
toast in the can-crushing lot, in the inside-out tomato
yards, where I am riding all the bicycles through
tunnels to the lawn, where I am on a downtown bus,
partially submerged, I am krill and various large birds,
the color grey of the sidewalk, a small opossum, in the
breaking glass in isolation in the sun, I am waiting for
the swamps and smoke of eucalyptus in the breeze, I
am stuck in traffic near the mudflats on the bay, I am
aimless and have several new tattoos.

————

Today I am rivets of sails in a log cabin where Jack
London lived in Alaska until they moved his cabin
here where we collect the change to buy our drinks
and eat the free hors d'oeuvres, where the neighbors
are somewhat pleased beside the railroad trains,
where the vague sense of the Union Pacific is with
opossums of freeways and you, where we've assembled
plastic birds all morning, where the airplanes fill the
plastic sky, where the fish are brightly colored on the
lawn, where an underwater bird is pummeled on the
sidestreet, where we take hallucinogens and wander
through museums, where the people construct the
artificial ponds, where theosophists arrive on all the
hillsides, where I have been bowling all morning,

where we have been airplanes and also the plastic
small birds, where this is the type of leisure that I am,
where these are the largest of fires, where the highway
trembles on the edge of the waterfront square.

————

I am collecting ceramic dogs and cats, I am awake
early today to go to the lawn from the shower to the
vacantest lot with all the pit bulls and the cars, I am
waiting for the man to come in through the window, I
am sitting on the roof devoured by the smog, I am
directing you to a sushi bar, I am cooking only foods
with milk and eggs, I am a tiny frozen squid.

————

I am here inside the freezer where you left me, I am
the unobstructed silence of the avocado dawn, I am
the neighborhood of foreign things, I am the
telemarketter of evening, I have only donuts and the
doors are locked, I am as thick as the morning down
on Broadway, I am walking near the freeway as it
shakes, I am the overpass and shattered in the midst
of day, I am the last of the partially submerged
vehicles on the waterfront on Sunday buying jam.

————

I am the waterfront and I cover the waterfront and all
the boats all know me, I am the foreignest of birds and
the shadows of sails upon martinis, I am underwater

buying jam and drinking stolen coffee, I am pelagic
now and sober, having recently discovered all the
birds.

———

I am not quite yet the harmony of spheres, I have
been hunting prey and building bridges for several
years now on and off, I am the foam of obstruction in
the foam of obstruction I am, I am the open bridge, I
am the falling away from a baseball game across the
earth on the edge of the islands and jail.

———

I am loving you beside the man with his pants down
on the highway where you are love itself and dying,
and from the inside of the train the subway tracks are
dangerous, I am dangerous and undangerous also and
a big shopping store I am, I am for the hillsides
bowling, I am unlike all the other counties in this
wood, I am clipped by cars while crossing major
streets, I am forced to wake at dawn and go to work
with all the pitbulls, cans, and coffee crushing lots, I
am the tiny specks of detritus and metal that flake in
the streets, I am the stray opossum at the undersides
of highways, I am the screaming man at midnight in
the lot.

———

As a community service offering I am stuffing
envelopes and studying the ties, I am here with the
opossums near the waterfront, I am wandering
unhindered by the food chain, I am fond of the can
crushing lot and ride my bike around it, I am at a
sidestreet fair still looking for Der Wienerschnitzel, I
am all tattoos and deejays, I am in love with the
parking lot, I am trying on new shoes, I am with these
murals of the cows in towns near towns and bridges.

———

Both sea lions and sea leopards cough in the halls of
our sleep while we play pinball, I am ebbing in and
out, I am dreaming dreams I hardly know and have
tattoos, I am dreaming dreams outside of dreams and
fish tanks and the spanishest of music.

———

In these tenements, inside this subterranean roadway,
upon this stream gone underground, from the top of
the hill and the door of the shoe store mid-town, I am
dreaming dreams I hardly know are dreams and in the
causeway, I am standing under the cracked bannister
observing all the parts, I am a subterranean cave
dweller clubbing fish, I have seen the light of day with
all the roaches, I have hardly noticed all the
artificialist lagoons.

———

I am standing on the corner where Huey Newton got
shot but you thought that he was Huey Lewis.

And especially from hot tubs at the parties with the
small ceramic cows and brie, astral-projecting, and
next to all comedians, from inside the t.v.s, to the
most exciting ocean, inside the several redwoods,
across the sparrows nesting in the porchlights on the
porch.

Where the mailman comes to, and so to the bridges
and tattoos I am, an albatross in the hottubs of dawn,
and so to the living room parents, and so to the
amazons who call me Lucretius.

I have been a long time in this story on the bridge
inside tattoos and wearing avocados, and I can think
only of myself, and I can steal the books in bookstores,
and I can collect cans at all the can and crushing lots,
and I am here to wait in line with others near the
lawns, and I am being shot at on the sidestreet, and I
am hording all the plastic pigs, and I am practicing
with others for the dawn, from rooftops where the
hills are all on fires with the most usual of
circumstances, where the fish are kept in large tanks
and a black smoke settles on the roof, where the

neighbors harbor pitbulls between the cars, where the
strange small apples bounce across the tar upon the
roof, where opossums cross against the flow of traffic,
where the streetlights blink and flicker on, where the
plastic and the airplanes fill the sky, where we live
beside the most chinese of oceans, where I gamble in
the empty and where winterless I am.

———

At dawn bent at odd angles the exercisers in the yard
speaking only dialects of fog, there were fish and then
tattoos, where we walked upon the waterfront of cave
bluffs, where the waterfront held shrimp, where there
were three dozen tourists behind the Thailand disco
beat, where the ferry left at dawn, where the buses
never came, where the sidewalk was all buckled,
where the customs seemed all strange, where I walked
in shadows of the eucalyptus night, where I seldom
rode in cabs, where I never owned a blue and shiny
truck, where you slowly bobbed your tea bag, where
the apple trees turned black, where I washed the fish
inside the fountain in the park, where I had been a
long time in this story on the bridge, where I have
been wearing avocados all day, where I am all tattoos
and dreams of fashion, across the glare of the roof,
near the church of Thelonius Monk, where I have
seen the soot upon the windows of tattoos.

———

This is a jumbo prawn and these are all the
mudskippers inside of rusted cans, these are the circles
underground revolving with the habitrails of squirrels,
this is a dangerous underground stream from which

we grow the underground tomatoes, these are the
tattoos of dawn, this is the tiny metal hatchet near
the bed, this is the sound of my television, that is the
sound of the tunnels of the highway.

———

Massive and damp, on the ell curve by the Cliff
House, next to the nude beach on the barrios that
point, where I used to like the Grateful Dead but now
I'm just a satanist, this is the Cafe Boheme where I
spend my time, these are the sneakers I'd like to look
cool in, this is the hallway with plantains and people
I know, these are my neighbors, that is the jukebox
place, these are the people who sleep on my steps, this
is the man in the laundromat who wishes he was
Carol Burnett.

———

I am bludgeoned by this most exotic ocean, currently,
I am in the post office with the prison cells and tides,
I am with the fires in the eucalyptus fog, I am clearing
and the colors are all changing, I am changing colors
in the lift of fog, I am almost to Japan, I am circles
and the squirrels revolve, I am missing plastic pets, I
am predictions of the sounds of tides and this.

———

I am this Santa Ana wind and we are bowlers, we are
at the haircut man, I have divulged so little of the
avocado dawn, I am waiting to buy coffee near the

docks upon the square, I am all the hot dogs and the
roof of city hall, I am hardly standing in the kamikaze
rain, I am of the new year sober now, I am inside of
all the horoscopes at once, I am the rainy part of early
fall expecting to go back across the bridges, I am near
the greenish plantains down the street, I am the
subtler angles of the sunlight from the surface of the
moon, I am here to yet predict the dawn, I am getting
better like the oceans on the sidestreet, I am
surrounded by water, I am walking sideways near the
church in Watsonville upon the orange line at
Lammas Tide.

———

This is from which I came expecting to see others, for
the others from which they came and came I in the
generations fog, from the fog of fog's tattoos, from the
avocado sunlight, from the avocados and the fog to
where I came, this is from where I came and to which
I came and from what I came down to the library, this
is from which then came the plantains of the dawn
and all graffiti, I came this way and this is from which
I came, and from the sun and from inside the tiny
plastic mammals, from this palisade and from this
palisade, from the advent of street preachers on this
block, from the church on the corner where I walk again
and sideways, from the countless vacant lots all
filled with eucalyptus trees, from this part of the walk
and at this angle, and from this stout and from the
top of this most certain hill, beside along and down
into our sleep, in these halls and only to our dreams,
from the surf upon the Cliff House, down the surge of
waterways in dark, of each condition from which I
came to come from with the avocado dawn, where I
am looking for Japan, where I expect the palisades to
fall, from inside of this Atlantis, from where we rise

like science, from where I walk down sidestreets with
a gun.

———

From the telemarketters of dawn to the wheatgrass
South of Market, in the sidestreet eating mushrooms
holding guns, for the greyish colored hills so patient in
the morning, for the stiffling avocados of the
subterraneanmost fish stores, for the shark's teeth on
the shore, for all half-eaten surfers, for the pier with
all the sink holes on the edge, for the most misplaced
of onramps, for the holding cells and gambling rooms
of dusk upon the fog.

———

I am holding the guns in the attics of downtown
stores and sewing buttons on the Neimun Marcus
pants suits, I am in the breakroom holding coffee with
my gun, I am asking you to help me, I am at the
ocean from the tops of towers with the murals of the
cows and factory workers paid for by the Coits, I am
watching all the tiny lights on all the hills go on and
off in darkness, I am waiting for catastrophes inside
t.v.s, I am jumping from the bridges tempted by the
waters far beneath, I am on the edge of Lucretius
where Peralta brought his cows to play pianos, I am
travelling by bus and I am travelling by horseback, I
am not sure where I am and I am travelling to edges
made of night, I am not sure where I am and I am
travelling to edges made of rock in avocado night, I
am travelling to the edges to the plane to where I am
to cross the parking lot to stand upon the median to
edges made of rock in avocado night.

Garrett Kalleberg

THE NEW GATE

to bind

to keep

to separate

to take in
like a gate, opening to concrete
fields, streams, states. At the edge

not shadow, not light —
forms moving, at the periphery forms

waiting. By the wall,
figures marching — in dark blue
or black — it is dark, too dark

to tell. It is hard to tell
one from another, gray
forms blocked out against a gray field,
as when one looks at a photograph
or map, a plan reproduced
in the newspapers — I seem to have
lost the clipping — what is ever left
anyway? The wall may be razed,
the plan remains.
The gate may be destroyed,

there will be a better gate
to stand the test — against which
all people move, though they may not know
where they're going.

Without obstacle,
the train pulls in — time
can be told by it — the new train
enters the gate,

but it does not go out again.
Following a straight line, bodies
enter in at the periphery.
But they do not go out again.

One could see, it is a good wall
and a good gate, opening

to a steady stream of gray figures, — nothing
is ever lost. Nothing has ever lived

and is lost to the mind which can

    receive

    divide

    hold

    bind,
as certainly as a concrete wall, a gate
or station — a state of rest
by a field of dead grasses.

INSIDE–OF–THE–BODY TEST

There will be one point for a correct answer
no point for no answer
and minus one point for every lie.
You will have five seconds to respond
five milliseconds
nanoseconds

revolutions of an electron
in a hydrogen atom
of a drop of water
in the vitreous humor of your right eye —
What's inside you, man? what's
keeping you alive! or is the question
too difficult, the eye
convoluted so
inward, on the repetition of one act
in the memory's
screen and all the individual
scenes become one   one
    cause
        which is the *real* cause,
heart   liver   spine   bowels   blood —
I must make a confession.
The senses bound to follow an inner
command, which is its own reward
even as certain thoughts attach themselves
to this image   tries to get out
and a muscle flinches
I could hit myself.

from *LIMBIC ODES*

I. MUTATION

Let me see you as you are

       like an eye in a field of sight.

Who made this eye?
What made this? to see
    thing AND / NOT thing.

Nothing made this to see.

To see
I made this eye
to see what is not seen
not things
but what holds them
that they are *as* they are
then it all changes, the eye
given new sight, the hand
new touch, the tongue a new
tongue and bones
reclothed in flesh which is the perfect
flesh of the body released
from the image which enslaves me.

The stiff body broken
to fit in the same room
as the body and become
gentler than he was
and become kind to animals
and become
and care

      the animals know
the smell of sickness
and the ants know
the body disrobed in earth
being human, and bones
broken to fit in the body and earth
broken to fit in the earth,

I open my eyes and see the fact, state, or
quality of being of a manner, way, or method
of doing or acting, or of the
of, belonging to, or associated with a specific
person, group, thing,
or category, appearance, form or
way of doing something or
the way in which a thing is done
or happens in which

an underlying substance or a permanent
way in which
something can be viewed
by the mind or attribute of that one
previously mentioned
is manifested.

When the sign is made present,
something disappears.
The reverse of this is also true.

"Decline, for perfection, or completion";
"prepared, for closed or concluded";
"withhold, for present, reveal, give"
something for nothing, the gift,
clearest blue sky, for the black
sun in the hole of the eye.

I am about 175 lbs. and
six feet tall; brown hair; blue eyes
and my name is blank
at the moment, imagine that
someday the name
will not hold. But it's hard to let go
of some things, and if I grow another arm
to take the place of my left arm — better yet
(because I am writing this with my right hand)
I am growing another hand
to take the place of this hand

but the arm is not an arm
and the hand is like a dead hand
or a painted one
or one made of stone
clinging to a stone
wall of endless
stone steps, leading
up to the art of the throat.
Now I am growing another throat

so that the poem will be more melodious
when read aloud — listen to this great sound
of a new angel
blown out of a horn
blown out of a bullhorn
the body is dead. This is the difference
between mouthing and saying
someone mouths, I bring it to life
by indicating a hand here
in the mouth of the bullhorn.

> I am afraid of this mouth,
> angel says,

> I am afraid of that hand
> ink says

and if the words are well-known, but the grammar
is yet to be explained
as when they make you take these things down,
but they don't tell you what they mean
or when in building, there is a beginning, middle,
and end, the work is done, there is something
where there was nothing, but I am not sure
that it is, and when you make
it up, so that it makes
some kind of sense — but the I has failed
in the one thing it was sent to do.

IX. AN UNDISTURBED SONG OF PURE CONTENT

There is a thing
or there are several things
which, recollected, are one thing
and this thing is a thought
or is a way of thinking
or is a way of undergoing
in the way that the tree grows

in the wind outside
the window, in the way that
the gate closes and footsteps are carried
down the street until the hand is frozen

in silence, then
scratches away again

away
the thing
goes away,
                    but then it comes back again.
                                                    The thing
can be torn off

                    like a piece of paper, or frayed

rope, or frozen hand clinging
clinging to the rope and so

particular, and so

real, existing, conscious of existing

between, and so
                    pulled between

            liquid and light

with its forehead pressed against the waves

until the wax is spent:

no history nor course
nor any end
but what is recollected

freely
            at an irremunerable price,

thing for thing.

In the aesthetic zone an angel
sounds a trumpet while the clothed
dead rise from tombs
       struggle from their shrouds
     rise whole from their tombs
          rise from the bellies of beasts
           are regurgitated from the bellies of beasts
are bones and parts in the bellies of beasts

                hunger
                for hunger
                of hunger
                after the thing, until it was ingested
                and become part of the body
                which is the whole
                hunger, until
                there was
                there will be
                not want.

The serpent devouring its own tail / The vomit unto God

which is the whole body / having no end

incorporating every part / for which the mind

universal theory must equally want:

The hunger of time devours the stars
which by the eye can be seen in imitation
of the suffering of every part.

The stars undergo
The angels undergo
and have developed their superior logic
to contain an excess of feeling

until they implode
in a pulse of light — the body transparent and weightless
will not be touched by fingers of dust
will not be divided into its constituent parts
of red and purple, — red — purple
in the field of light in the ground of blackest
ether, dead as phlogiston
the particles do not necessarily return

and do not necessarily
go away again. And if they wait, and want, though
knowing not what?
but wanting must take an object.
Hunger of prehistory
and the unhappiness we have known
in our own days
              even unto our own days

I want
not of hunger of prehistory
and the unhappiness we have known
in our own days, we
whom I call
you whom I call upon with
you to whom I
and you to whom I
you alone, who

you, and the other
you divide until
flesh of God
is consumed in
flesh of worms,
remains when the white and translucent
flesh of the body
remains warm to the touch
even warm to the touch
and all I touch

and not its parts
I fear, that have
no fear of death the whole
of death, and not its parts
unfolding, opening up, emptying out
in the present moment though you
hear me speaking, saying
I say
nothing
not a thing not
thing not
not thing.

Candace Kaucher

EX POST FACTO GOD

Reciprocal effacement
(ie: nothing to attach it to)
duel wormholes inviting
and so ruining the vacation
hatracks of their pleasure:
I wore a dunce cap labeled love
like minimalist sculpture safe
passage from the realm of glittered banners
mistaken for end purpose.
Then I am the message in motion not to
register as braille interference –
out across the marketplace cinematic concrete abutment ear
become confused with undulation.
Eagerly, this body patrols the surface
its crunch apparent stasis
solution to solidity or
dreadmill with a thousand takers.
Whose weavings is your love.
Whose summation equals scream
pinpricked with the most silent of consciousnesses
on one hand expansive on the other imposed.
If motion could be considered
the crenelated capsule of confinement
this is where we have taken shelter:
(They're not letting anything grow.)
between walls as whispered secrets
lapsed pubic gardens of stone.
Whereupon all the absurd fracturing
center of protracted illusion
implanted in my eminence grinds
to recreate the dreaming figurehead.

SWALLOWED OPINIONS BUT GOOD ONES

The kitchens churn out the faces of little boys
who don't know they're somebody's echo
or a milkshake in a monk's hammock,
a sperm with a religious sealing on it.
They're whistling babies in their dragnet booties
as all the dregs come seeding up from the mantra side of town,
butt heads on the microchip playing field.
The macrocosmic essay is out of focus too, for a larger reason,
since there is no place for me to set my lunchbox.

New meaning seems to be cropping up everywhere
like a gadfly on a garbage scow.
It's a black hole bulimic on a diet of emptiness
with just the demon sided page flapping in
an unfettered step to the next day's affairs,
a sad box of carnivals accustomed to shining
brightly in the lap of commodity.

Without such pleasantry of the maniacs
what kind of sanity would you call this
truncated atrophied underworld dream dimension chaff
from the legs of love's patrons pealing
in the soundless project:
a conversion table calibrated to recoup
any variance between decision
and the pitiful parody of it.

But like all sad cops of the ministry
he has to learn to kiss the stone contrived ambiguity
until absence or negation read like a label
of quality merchandise from a name brand store
only in a galaxy you never heard of.

It even wants to be your lover.

VIRGINIBUS PUERISQUE

Pleasure dresses the means
of our pain flowing cinematic
eight ball of bronchial dust.
A disassembling hack
wrenches half the world
into a locked device,
and the other
half's lingered in tension's
flailing magma prison
too long.

No flowers for me
to pluck out of existence
when rituals are costly
and the sand painting's
already gone out on the carpet.
You never do get to compare notes.

After all, subjects
in the lab tests proved inconclusive
like islands and continents
playing chess in an ocean
of puritanical jack move;
I motion and plasma becomes manna.

Instant replay
and one suddenly becomes expert
in case the rule of restriction
tightens up our belts
for one last hit (noxious
stupor you can't dream
the championships of because
it would be too boring
for a low dig high brow
to appreciate).

Nonsense is about all there's left to believe in.

An ability to reconstruct
a face, as it is deforming,
as it turns, as everything
does, into clouds.

CHLOROFORMS

To frolic gaily in behavior,
to force in utterly all of you
ravaged by the foreignness of your sequence
tripping shaft to the condom's scent,
I take you into my hands, literally wrench
organs into submission
and a meaning into this existence.
I mean if I asked you to disrobe
to the metaphysically soothing order of opium
it's not a multiplicity for us.
It's an ontological omnibus,
and we're high steppin it over the crosswire
planet, all polyethylenes and baggage:
as mutable obelisk of nomenclature.
Your oppressor well dressed
as redemption changes comic frame
crowding out the megabytes
until the winter emerges disheveled,
carelessly tossed behind
the duck blind, pressed
up against fin de siecle glass
with treasure map stuffed tightly
into singularity of purpose.
If not for extraneous noise,
sometimes, I wouldn't even
know I was on this planet
of plastic name tags.
That's the problem.
You've strung your mask together
like the passing scent of libationary garbage

on idiot breeze of moron notion.
My rat burst open
into flowers, mortal & immoral,
that cry in the shape of your merriment
beaten by choke hold leashes
to submission, and mellow dramatically
mediocre decked out slip shod clairvoyant momentary
slope and smiles of the antidote Utopian.

THERE IS ONLY SO MUCH SPACE IN TIME
— or —
OH BOY!   TRANSFERENCE

How much more joyous
could the people
in the little steeple houses
get before cuts mend.

This is gratitude silly rabbit

A wizard aloft in a stupid doorway
an elementary social crisis
a butt headed bee brained
media slain punked century . . .

The pain, the dream, the spit

And so we stick like karma
stuffed way far up Xion's
buffed and powdered pretty little ass
as remaining members of history
come pouring out of the cloakroom
heart deep on language psychosis,
a nest full of vagabonds and Times
Square cue cards see I'm cashing
in on irony, right now.

Dancing within the vertical hold
where eternity is that
widening gyro spire
only Yeats is allowed to talk
about
attitude
already
eating you.

MOLECULAR VISCOSITY

Say an emptier heart makes more music
than the senseless ruse of complacency.
Its homogenous quatrefoil finely leafed
in answer to seamless nothings,
angst to razor's edge.
Crowded by the dredge of blunt resistance
only just learning how to spell
the Archemidian leverage point
strummed continuously like life
stolen from a Brandenburg Concerto
and slandered to sublimity.
Anesthetic litanies in love
with the impossibility of ecstacy
like hood ornaments ripped off
from a handbag clutched frequency
patented as anonymously as a myopically grandiose
vacuum trained ever encyclopedic
politely lipped wine glass,
like any static that obscures.

PERCEPTUAL DISTANCE

And the wiring alone is enough to unnerve one.
The strip of this street with a line no soul could follow.
Bowels of pipeline underneath mime the glass mirage
Hovering in space twenty feet off

In the window memorex.
A city full of peace in a containment field,
Readying itself for orders
(your orders)
Like each and every flight of fancy, hung
Immediately above the throng of bodies
Cramming the medium street.

To be sure somewhere in the solution a transparency
Was developing — name space left blank too
For all manor of signature:
A construct of binary code that the streetlights could be
If the people were positioned with rocks
At precisely the right moment.

Almost as if spectral cities acquired a defaulted language.
And a letter came drifting down from any penthouse
Stuttering on the swell like its own semaphore code.

If one could view in insect infrared — the sublimity
Every chimera hopes to possess —
The antimatter of desire would seem a play dough blur
Of colors kept unsegregated and swirled into one interbred
Hue bled prism song. Except the paddy wagon shop windows
Are so used to this to have developed an abrasion
That only spits back untenable portraits of the prestige
That wishes it were walking by.
And the only soul emerging,
A sequined red dress of passionately burning business sense,

Puts out a blank facade of TV screen
Unwilling to throw its whispered plastic to do
Dull beta radiator foul lover's groan and will.
Ready to drown you just as you come upon wispy steam.
It has a new contract not to disappear —
Proximity won't mean a thing.

ODE THROUGH GRAVITY TO SPACE

Only your aspirant amateur landscape
might capture pears
splattered in a painterly drone.

Across the mirror of hype
its tonic painfully lubricates
life beat into video andante

with numbness that refuses to spit up
its terror even though it's choking on it.

In the drawings you see
love disappearing into a mountainous lavender

as if certainty was
a trestle that wants to blow out
separating you from the sea you don't deserve.

Not a chaotic sound crawls through
any window of a citizen.
So stealth injects humanity into its machine
like tiny little actors
at arms with the alphabet in your chest.

An imperceptible pink hemorhage
cloned perimeter still life
unfolds in senseless meditation.

Time awakens beside itself

and we squirm, or at least you do.

PHAINETAI MOI (Sappho)

It appears to me that his godhead
divines your little one on one.
He plays forward on the sweet phone
of your acuteness

and galling desirability.
This is my cardiac chest unfeathering.
When I see you, nothing comes
to me to speak.

My tongue is broken. Straightway
a fine flame consumes my skin.
With my eyes I see nothing and hear
forebodings of rain.

A cold sweat downs me. A trembling
seizes all. I am more green than
grass time. I am dead no less
than I appear.

HOI MEN HIPPEON STRATON (Sappho)

Most men take strategic knights, while others
claim armymen; the rest hold up battleships
as the greatest show on earth. But I declaim.
It's who do you love.

It's no trouble to cinch this once and for all.
For she was Helena, beauty of the mortal
elsewhere, who left the man, the aristocrat,
behind.

And went floating off to Troy, with no
mind for offspring or beloved parents.
Love walked her sideways, knowing
straightway.

For swayed
      lightly   t   one
      puts me in mind of Anaktoria, now
out of sight.

I would rather see her step the lovely
and do the facial shine more than any
continental chariot decked with soldiers
under arms.

WINGS OF LOVE (Simias)

Look, I'm the ruler of deep-sternumed earth; sky took a seat elsewhere.
Don't tremble if the chin of so small a being is dark with curls.
For ego was generated on the way back when Necessity ruled
all creepers of earth must defer to baneful decrees;
all, even those creeping
thru air.
Of Chaos
am I called the child;
I'm not the swift-winger of Aphrodite and Ares.
For I reign not with force, but with persuasive logos.
They defer to me, earth and sea of hollows and heaven bronzed.
From them I snaked the ogygian sceptre and gave orders to the ordainers.

ALTAR (Besantius)

The wet gore of holies
does not dye me purple
with infusions of red.
The knives honed on the Naxian stone spare
the folds of Pan; the fragrant resin of Nysian
sticks darkens me not with its curling smoke.
You see in me an altar made neither
with Aurian bricks or Alubian clods.
Don't put me on a scale with the one
built by the Kynthos born duo
who took up the horns of
bleaters, however many feed
on the smooth ridges of Kynthos.
The earthborn 9 made me with
the descendants of heaven,
their everlasting art validated
by the palm of the immortals.
o drinker of sources chiseled
open by Gorgon's son, may you
sacrifice and liquidate me with
libations more sweet than
those of the Hymettians. Come and be stout
on my fabric, for I am free of the venom
sent by the monsters who lurk around the one
near Myrina in Neanian Thrace, the one the thief
of the purple ram set up to you, triple patronizer.

EGG (Simias)

check this

of a warbling mother

you get ready for a holy heart

herald of gods Hermes tossed it rioting

from monaural metric he bid the count wax full

above he gave the sign for a quick slant of scattered feet

changing limbs with hasty fawns varied tokens of the lightfooted deer

all go tearing with feet on a peaceful nursing mission over high mountains

then some wildhearted beast gets the call sounding in deep recesses of chamber

tuning in the cry of sound he drives for snowbeaten range straightway to leafy dell

stirring those swift feet like these manifold measures the renowned god let loose the song

leaving rocky bed he rushes swiftly bent to snatch an errant token of the dappled mother

sounding thru ranges of fattening sheep they go to the caves of slender ankled nymphs

with immortal desire for a nourishing breast they rush to their lovely mother

striking out the glitter on the trail of the much varied Pierian song

to a great peak of ten footers out dealing kosmos for rhythm

to the mortals from under lovely mother's wing

a mother's shrill throes worked it out

a Dorian nightingale

new warp

VANILLA

The beautiful bird talk is certainly a form
of your tastebuds & fleshly lips. Verily
your delicates flavor a teaspoonful in combination.
The fan shape adds an extra boost. Coloring
also enters into it. At this point I am unfocused
by all the melting. Your ice cream face
and numerous aerial hairs make my heart
beat against the spikes of lucky stars.
This to me is pure vanilla extract.

SWING

As visions go, you take all the nines
and dress them. More than a few angels
are needed to match your excellent wardrobe.
For you have special outfitters to deal and deck
your lovely form. Bubbles of conditioner give you
a fresh canopy of real ease but true light is thrown
from beneath your outer bloom. Those upper middle
bones take the turn of the beacon. The pearl shines
in a mark of oval tender. For the most part I am
not in my skin. There can be no more sight
after your fashion show. The unfurling lotus
breaks pike in glass. Everything hurls for the
delicious. Let us play through and reach the stick.

MILLEFLEUR

To have "been away," the summer erodes
into a glistening length as green stone
bobbles float
on the surface of a paper
back book of
"poetry."
While I was away you were knotting
the white string
into confabulations, I see,
and underneath the Scandinavian beige
color
a sunset reoccurs serially

not so much as to enliven the supermarket
parking lot
but to stun us with gratitude and
astonishment.
To have been away
as though folded into an intercession
looking for the glimmer
that is your signature fruit
as not any pomegranate studded with
ruby nails
will do.
Did you know that carnations
symbolize Christ, Iris's "the Virgin"
and a chinese lantern "life in death"
as perceived in a millefleur,
a threaded canopy hung with
linden where
lie the shoemaker and his love
in the burnt red color of a late
October afternoon

in the north
where dusty particles
make the night an even
sheen, an enclosure of rocks.

I can't quite tell you where I've been.
Someday I'll write somebody a letter maybe.
It was like walking in a marsh of frogs

or pulling from under roots
of a tree

strange and terminal

like at the ferry

a green round room flooded with
the station's light
the disclosures of the brain
as rapid and delineated as an
M&M's wrapper wrought into who
knows what design and discarded
into these ideas of reference.

A white bone fence
he wore
around his neck
or maybe it just seemed that way

as a fence could be a necklace
of a kind
as the skin slips through
its jelly slipcover

free to be born.

You who
holds the flower's

gestating capillaries, perception's
branches and jewels.

EON

There is the wobble of rain.
After the blue emanation,
soba noodles, bent daffodils, and songs
emerge like a needle
from the windy fire,
cavalcade of horses and rocks.

In this anthem the moon
is a white fin that rigidifies in our iris
and hollows the mouth
that invokes, like a pump,
the five black stairs
to the ravine.

"Watchtowers of the North"
are compressed on the horizon
as those whitish trees between the Sonoco
sign and glaze of humidity
buckle the page.

I came to it with my mouth open,
half loaded.

The sonic dimension
was like this car that actually said:
"the door is ajar, the systems intact."

Now the goof balls will charge
the alabaster
tinges
and the classic will arise
cool as ice-cream
portable as the sun.

Sometimes it seems all of life
is this relentless machine
ordering you to its duty
but that's my excuse because I go
compliant as a maenad (Roman copy of a
Greek original)
head bent to the thyrsus
a mechanic with a flashlight.
All of the field is a warm
beige haven, a nothingness of particulars
punctuated by dinky Christmas tree lights
and the measured dance of transparent figures
around a glass vase
wedged in between a manila envelope
containing itself: the obstetric.

Women Working Wool (540 B.C.)
share this field
plaiting the strands of talk
tying off the clusters
in geometric black dresses
in front of a weird, sunset colored space.
We go down to the Shohola
and the cool snakes
that inhabit the ledges
retreat slightly.

Immersed in its vault
night is spare, emits its messages
peripherally. How the rocks on the plank
feel as you pass by, wet as a dog,
remade by its fluorescence.

For instance: something happens.

The crack of rifles on the porch
as men in wool pants
aim their guns.

The divination wobbles then,
the ephemeral energies
of their traces
laid on the air and elm trees
gravitate to where hands hold the glass
and are asked the questions that have to be
asked.

How ever this room got made, the perspectives
rotate
so as each wall is a universe
of ordering nodes
and a cat will chase a snake will bite the bee
in days to come watch and see.

It was a place, rumored to be a cairn,
some kind of underground bunker bar
in which out of work guys hunker down
and all of the textures are off kilter
and damp. The curtains
are printed with miniature spuds and elks
that chase the bride down the hill
into a minty vale
and a mighty blue nighttime.
But when we drove up
the neon hissed through the rain.
A man who had met the pope the day before
tried to sell us a grandfather clock.
Later I took that as some kind of indication

that time is cultural,
organized along corporate lines
chopped up any old way that serves the
dominant ideology, dressed up
in clogs, nails, and
bandages, the transparent linen
threads loosely folded to resemble
hair
but peering through the rags at the portal

there was only the ancient slime beloved
to its manufacturers and useful as a
lubricant.

A whirling vortex of fragmented conversations
threw off sparks, shards
of the beautiful shale
that banks the old road
and all of the big wet leaves,
triangular blades, lie on the pavement
as though positioned by the black figures
working wool
to be read as a copious text

reverberating echoes
off of the other centuries and
written to keep us
writing the next.

If you break an alphabet
and place it in a circle
let Eon choose
its reconfigurations, the long sentence
out of the mouth
the mouth of the universe all
projectile, sequence, and charms
that vibrate multidimensionally.
The currents
a magician's
punctuation.

Okay, some take mystification
and make it magic.

Like the fluid shape of
an enormous body
enclosing the Shohola's detritus,
the water
holds her as she passes underneath us,

a mirror that
contains negation and desperation.
Eon's breath on our hands
scrambles the cubes
and makes new words as the old alphabet,
syllables of identity, erode in the flicker
of a fire that lines the path.

I stood by a funny
old bedroom lamp of brown paper
and green ceramic horses
examining the latch on a red purse
when you came in. We talked about
the perimeters
that seemed to
be as transparent as dragonfly wings
and just as tactile and expansive
but there was also this sense
of a vocabulary diminishing
around the core of feeling
that generates
this molecular vibrancy. I sat
on the bed
picking at white chenille,
the workings of his face a book
while the letters hilariously run away

because as night comes on
even the furniture slopes
and there's a multiplicity of objects.
There's too much of everything,
more than the amount with which we started.

Our love
becomes a sweeping plum
atmosphere
elements attend.

This exhaustion
elastic and stable
yields recognition
of narrow, billowing shapes,
electrical snaps
along the line
as you approach
discernible entities,
monstrous, beloved
manifestations.

At the instant
of equivalence,
the radio starts up with that
haunting music from Afghanistan, love duets.
The clock seems to literally
wring the hours dry and
screws them back
onto the ramp
and we have many things to tell you
of the flood,
the low-ceilinged room with gun racks
and a string hanging from the ceiling
and a daddy longlegs
walking on the rim of the toilet.
The photograph of twelve dead deer
lined up for a portrait on the snow.
There is a continual crackling that comes
from the woods in the morning
and later you realize it's the sky that scratches
their name, the Lanape, indecipherable
as a stem that's lost most of the leaf
but they are buried in the ground out there.
She sleeps under a painting of two women
who sit in chairs
in ornate lace gowns, an artery of blood
ties them together like a clothes line in the
backyard wind.

Although this is a specialized space
that ties us to them, the twins,

as if it was a wholeness,
a way of keeping in sight everything,
all of the edges as you focus
on the middle as
the sorting process begins,
chambered until the day
its innate spectral beatitude
and lamentation flows through us.

Inside a circle of glasses
from the bodega, white candles.
To articulate the effect
of a motion just passed through as
receding frames of the thresholds,
you feel freaky,
encapsulated in cognition and substance
inside the great, driving lucidity.

To move around and situate
is just so many lost repetitions, a dry mouthed
ballet against irreducible solids.
Finally, you let yourself
be put aside gradually as
a partition. The content
held in the body
as provisional a filter as that is.

A web, a curtain
of filaments
how the matching motions of the
other
partially seen
sequence the chain.

Nothing might jerk the other side
just as likely
but since the jug rounds
you never do see
all of its content at one time.

Jeffrey McDaniel

THE QUIET WORLD

In an effort to get people to look
in each other's eyes more,
and also to appease the mutes,
the government has decided
to allot each person exactly one hundred
and sixty-seven words per day.

When the phone rings, I put it to my ear
without saying hello. In the restaurant
I point at chicken noodle soup.

I am adjusting well to the new way.
I have placards for every occasion.
Each morning, I invent a new phrase
which I print on a t-shirt,
like *The Humans Are Coming*
or *Karaoke For Mutes.*

Late at night, I call my long distance lover,
proudly say *I only used fifty-nine today.*
I saved the rest for you.

When she doesn't respond
I know she's used up all her words
so I slowly whisper *I love you*
thirty-two and a third times.
After that, we just sit on the line
and listen to each other breathe.

OPPOSITES ATTACK

I walk on tiptoes so as not to disturb
the elderly couple sleeping quietly
on the floor. Outside the sky is the color
of a drowned man's face. The birds
are still on strike. The local children
build a snow transvestite. The trees have rolled
up their long sleeves. They're cousins
with the octopus. I remember packing snowballs
in the ice box and dreaming
of beaning sunbathers in July. I was never good
at sunbathing. I used to climb the fire escape
and recline on the roof's rough blanket at midnight
pretending the house was a wedding cake
as I covered my limbs with cooking oil
and offered myself to the moon.

Those were the good, cold days, when a Peeping Tom
was actually worth something, and a wise crack
got you a kick in the pants. Nowadays
you need an Glock in the glove compartment
and a cavalry of narcotics galloping
through your veins, just to get a police officer
to spill coffee on you, and sometimes
even that isn't enough. I see
your cross-eyed pigeon and raise you a jar
of epileptic brains. Put your business cards
on the table. Read the palm trees
and weep. Roman numerals weren't built
in a day. I bet you an opera singer's esophagus,
my apocalypse can beat your apocalypse
even on an off day.

THE OFFER

I want to locate a bit of you, cradle it,
say: this, there is no word for this.

But they will. They who name everything
will define our actions
as we auction our bodies off to sleep.

In our single dream we'd compose
a manifesto on the irregularity of scars.

The very idea demands preparation, as if
choosing a school for an angel.

There are no angels. Just those things
blinking like the teeth of jackals
around the moon's significant tremble.

Isolate the idea of shaking our bodies
under the blank comfort of down and tell me
which way will our knuckles face?

Now shake the idea of our isolated bodies
as the sheets become our Miro.

If you stay, the walls will admit their cracks.
See it forming, already on their lips.

D

When the sun was a child's breath above the Earth
you were the one I turned to
wearing something dark and celestial
like the sky over Colorado.

You were elegant, like a night stick
balanced on the tip of a steeple

and seductive, like watching an archer
untie her bow.

You were the one I trotted back to, like a horse
with a bell around my neck
and dangerous, like polishing the horn of a ram.

You rendered me crazy, like the footprints
of a husband chasing his wife
with a garage door opener through the snow.

You were mysterious, like a chandelier
suspended by a rattlesnake.

Your palms were the islands
of sleep I swam between.

A kiss with you was like driving off a cliff
clutching a sawed-off telescope.

When I split, pain spread through the rumor
of my body like truth.

Knees turned to powder in their caps.

I rolled back and forth on the floor
like a four syllable word.

Every child I looked at
began coughing uncontrollably.

Every building I entered
became the house of separate beds.

Here is a bag filled with the vowels
that tumbled out of me.

Here is the sand castle I destroyed
with the limb of a friend.

Here is the sound of a hero
outgrowing his confetti.

Here, where the stars are scraps of metal
holding the world in place.

FIRST PERSON OMNISCIENT

I made her tell me of the affair,
    every detail,
and I became him, the man who pulled
    her into the closet,
opening the many rooms of her mouth,
    knobs spinning,
and then I was her, pulling him
    by the tongue
through the river of rooms in the mansion
    of my mouth,
his eye pressing into me, his eye
    seeing all,
and then I was the closet, the space
    they traveled through
on their way to the mansion, and then the real
    I entered the closet,
the wind of doors slamming, bodies
    rushing, gone —
my eye lost in the mouth of my pocket,
    or is it my hand,
my dirty, awful hand.

EXILE

Mathematicians still don't understand
the ball our hands made, or how

your electrocuted grandparents made it possible
for you to light my cigarettes with your eyes.

It isn't as simple as me climbing into the window
to leave six ounces of orange juice

and a doughnut by the bed, or me becoming
the sand you dug your toes in,

on the beach, when you wished
to hide them from the sun and the fixed eyes

of strangers, and your breath broke in waves
over my earlobe, splashing through my head, spilling out

over the opposite lobe, and my first poems
under your door in the unshaven light of dawn:

Your eyes remind me of a brick wall
about to hammered by a drunk
driver. I'm that driver. All night
I've swallowed you in the bar.

Once I kissed the scar, stretching its sealed
eyelid along your inner arm, dried

raining strands of hair, full of pheromones, discovered
all your idiosyncratic passageways, so I'd know

where to run when the cops came.
Your body is the country I'll never return to.

The man in charge of what crosses my mind
will lose fingernails, for not turning you

away at the border. But at this moment
when sweat tingles from me, and

blame is as meaningless as shooting up a cow with milk,
I realize my kisses filled the halls of your body

with smoke, and the lies came
like a season. Most drunks don't die in accidents

they orchestrate, and I swallowed
a hand grenade that never stops exploding.

THE MULTIPLE FLOOR

Christmas. Again I desert my younger brothers
with freaks disguised as our parents
yanking them back and forth in the snow.

I won't unwrap anyone's expensive feelings for me.
My darkest thoughts dangle from my ears.

An oxygen mask is an abandoned building
neighborhood children learn to breathe in.

A suitcase is what a father carries
down the staircase of broken plates.

I walk through Manhattan, following the footsteps
of God running out on the world.

On Houston Street, a person rattles in a box
like a present so horrible even the wind won't open it.

Glorious and *getting worse* sound the same to me.

Innocence is a finger coming off
in a glove during a snowball fight.

In Tompkins Square, a fiend ties his arm
with Christmas lights and plugs in his only tree.

Panic spreads its hideous cream over the cheeks
of a statue. and I used to be that statue.

I hoist a pale vowel up the throat's pole,
wave it in surrender over the body.

CHIVALRY

A woman asks to borrow my salt
but I know what she wants: me to juggle

goldfish around her bed while she dreams.

It's gonna take more than two buttons
unsnapped on that smile.

Please?

Who does she think she is, *pleasing*
for my salt in public?

I feel powerful, moral.

She folds up her sleeve, exposing
a tattoo of a goldfish.

No one sees. I nod.

She peels the bronze carp
from her bicep and swallows.

If you want salt, beg.

In the polished tusks of her calves
walking away, I see myself: transmogrified,

pure and glossy.

Hands pressed. Knees together.
I can't stand up.

INVIGORATED SIGHT

1.

The ease astonishes by which
you cover miles to a threshold
where poet and scientist stand
on a wide beam at moonrise.

Now I find your thought beside me.
Tomorrow, I expect to see you on the hill
going toward your mistress Poesie —
the flag drops down like Quixote's lance.

My house is your house
Guillaume Apollinaire
and it is simple and deep
because you built it.

You began the century with a halloo
that goads us now at the finish.
Gunfire lights up the desert —
our cities are racked with it —

which did not stop your tongue
from recovering to tell us
of the spirit of the poets to come
and we are not now defeated.

Providence is the city of poets,
Guillaume Apollinaire.
This grass is your green imagination
you left it for me to walk on.

2.
Gardens in Kingston
come back in the French Poets
because of their city, Paris,
made of plants, water, and light.

The paths have been touched by sun:
the ranks of azaleas, old men at croquet
in the *jardains*. I pick one stone (an opal)
and fix it to my sleeve for art's sake.

Kingston: the Hope Gardens
a reservoir for all types of green
moss, invigorated hedges
blaze of the poinciana in July

flamingoes in a green pool —
of course they stand on one leg
winged veterans from the First World War
as I think of Apollinaire, you

poet of the written image
poet of the fountain that speaks
poet of melancholy advance
poet of invigorated sight.

The children are here.
They come for the flamingoes
and it is as you said
that the gardens are open for them.

MORE THAN ONCE IN CAVES

Once, fast along the ridge, we stopped where bush opened
The bones in a pit eager to enter the fuselage of our talk
The swerving of terrain, awake to the measure, the iron of its eye
I tried to pick out the moment when calm went south
And you the girl beside the ridge, a huge breadfruit tree

With balls of fruit, like soccer balls, the pimples are also green
I came from the tree and stood beside you like a vine
To crawl upon the main trunk where the sun sat like Jesus

Once, in deep anguish, the ridge buckled and left us
Steel pipes ran beside the cave where we made fishhooks
Of bone, the debris living with us, a rock with blood on it
The tableau with ankh to protect our backs from the heat
O thief I went home from the ridge, a mountain lion
Circling the wood pit, the cave was of bone, the fire not yet come
To dynamite the hill as we angled toward its mouth
I waded among the splinters of a water fight, out on to Crete

Once, in archipelago, a necklace tied with water, a fuse lit
Brought us into the cave, it shut like a footlocker on our plight
Forced to huddle, we waited for a fire, we sucked gas
And dreamt of smoke and drew pictures of copulation, I went
Beside salt marsh in Guinea, or under stars, of the roof hole
You brought in dyes and set paintings on our left
The rooms lie still, the noise of your breathing in my head
Man in a cave beside a fish bone hook, woman beside a cave

Once, we saw that it was night, the cave opened out of a hill
The rains came, and phonemes sprang new from the ridge
People left for grasses east of the Nile, and I was left
A shell of crab on my back, a crop of wool for my head, gear
Of lights deep over the grass, we ate from each other's hand
Choice meats were stored beside the pit of wood for your trek back
And I took to my bed in thorn, and rain wet me from the roof hole,
Next day we planted out a canefield, I begged you to hand me up

Once, when begging was invented, we sat out the fire and winded
I touched your palm print to my palm for the need of a self
The cave beside a mound of slag, we made hooks of iron from this kiln
The salt mines of Liverpool, the coal pits of Dahomey, the benches
Of courts with smooth bars for the plea, you on the steps
I went up to you when begging was the norm, when the cave was burnt
Poking through the ash, you to the camp of refugees, I to the holding pen
The men went out to plant with their hands what grew in that place

Once, I returned from your neck where my face was on fire
To dig up the roots that grew under earth at the earthworm's back
I picked apples with the daughters of sons, I bought a transistor radio
To you I gave every penny of my sweat till the plantings were done
I looked at sun, straight at it for once, to see if I could stand god's mouth
Went east with the cargo of my doubt, the cave was flooded
We turned back then, to snow beside the hooks made out of our
     colloquies
There were five of us: two of us were mules, three men in a cave

How easy to be alone when the wind insists, the bones we collect
As easy as digging up the hole, the spirals of talk you make out of wind

from *MOTH-WINGS*

PANEL ONE: ADVENT OF THE HILL

The word — the husk — splits open, and out crawl tiny black ants, each
with a piece of the man. I am scattered among these ants; like them, I am
become part of a trail that moves, joining the hill to the garden.

Left behind by the rain, a puddle in the dug-up earth. A dead moth in the
puddle. What, I wonder to myself, will happen to this moth, the colors on
its wing all bright in death?

     o

When the sun sets, the leaves whirl in the yard with force, and the rustle
is of feet in the wood, countless words. The whispering of faded memory.
Faded people walking hand in hand, admiring the beauty of the wood, the
naked branches overhead, like the wings. Faded words, and well used,
taken up and turned over by the hand.

Out in front of me, a flickering moth still in sight of the orchestra, smaller
than a blade of grass, of an earth color, mingling with scraps of rust. The
iron wing-drift of the moth. The uncanny present of the moth, big with
effort, dense.

The ants come to haul us to a section of the hill-nest they use for debris. All the words are there, black and red, long words and short, foreign words and familiar, piled up in a heap — of unbleached rice. Dead ants next to the moth, which is dead, and the languages thin from overwork. We carry them to the foot of the hill. We come up from the cellar. The line from the hole to the hill, to dirty puddle with the moth, and back to the hole, the nest. I am at the outer part of the nest.

The hill is a vessel for the ants. Who will fill it once it empties for the night? The storm of ruin comes to our house. The storm of a common day. And the body lies broken on the hill, the weaver-woman spent, and the ants with rice in their jaws. The mirror lies face down, in the garden. The body in time, moving from grass to grass. I am with the ants, black among the red, no longer drinking from the light, no light leaves, all is black, for now. Or not even black, no more than common. The whole yard springs from the tree, the roots of the tree meeting in the trunk, and branching into sky and fruit.

The dancers have all gone under the hill.

PANEL SEVEN: NOTES FOR A BOOK ABOUT DANIELLE

morning, dirt — febrile and absolute, uncanny

one into many; sherds of the self; on the turf

edges of the light, facing out again, to the black

a fracturing of person, place, thing — a grammar of the self

delving backward, where the scraps, coalesce and reassemble — odd search and the shelf

aspects — facets of travel; recognition of the two-point plan; one way to loss

shock of the loss — that there could be such a bird

sweet blossoms on asphalt of the engine

here and there, a mobile breakage; effort to collect some thing

probing through to fever grass in the mist

surprise of finding an empty lot, a broken bicycle, a kid

recall; roll call to see what happened; who steps up when called

all this and more, people from the mist, a crowd, a field

poverty of coming back to the lot; to the shops: palace in a smoky light

dense brush at the bath, reservoir where messages come; I take a long
look

a sense of wreck to be overcome by hypothesis

hypothesis about a yard where two stand sufficient, dense

not static — an interchange, a flower

entering and mixing, dying off, resurging, becoming over and over, with
heats and desire of stand

a story — an abstraction from story, of a trip

of desire thwarted, pushing out, but kept in, kept away from the condi-
tions of its lot

a case of the spume that plays upon the ghostly paradigm of things

bodies of the cave, the light projects shadows of the bodies — olive trees
in Greece, mango trees in St. Thomas — on the window of the wall

a teaser of desire to become form; a flash on the minutiae of cement;
sealed mouths open

but light, daylight to the white, the colorless, the bright light

but before this light

golden-thighed one, Pythagoras

and a story to tell, everything that causes it, from where they come to a fork, and then separate, like air from lungs

a wind of monstrosity — break break break

cold stones, the sea

o

The reservoir as a cliff. A massive problem of logistics to get it right. Smooth sides for all of that. A circle.

And the blazing heat if you stand in one place, a dangerous solitude, and irreversible.

Sister to the bigger basin where the shore coughs up froth. Jagged teeth of the moon on sea, of the coast.

Nights of violent celestial events — a suicide of rats in a net, heaven vomits up scraps of flesh, you and me together with our heads down.

I can't stand it. Can you explain to me why you did that? How much gasoline to the next motel?

The axiomatic — atomic fury of the clouds and our terror. How it crashes in over my head.

The blaze of the guns. Trenches down your front. We should have been born before the sky went dead and the hullabaloo took away our nerve.

In short, we were happier than dogs, but only for a while. Only the circle of night can outlast the hallucination of the good, the rivers of light. (The night.)

PANEL EIGHT: INTERLUDE

You require some explanation. You think, perhaps, it was not right to tell it like that, the sentences so depleted of juice. It was nine months ago. A delphic nightingale sits in the branches of the forest at Dodona, and this is what it says. *Circles pricked through with cones, and the seed of perishing also the seed of light.* How else could it be? I had washed up on the sand, outside the taxonomy of the biologists — outside the possibilities of syntax to express. I was a beast, the enemy of the birds. The way one fine morning you're asked to pretend you're a snake, and everyone gets down on his stomach and slithers and gets dirty. Some ridiculous change had overtaken my life. I stopped going out of the house for any reason. I lay quiet on the floor, day after day, eating slices of bread and nothing much else, ignoring the telephone, the heaps of mail, and the knocks on my door at all hours. Things could have gone on like this, indefinitely, except that one day, I looked up and saw that the weather had turned bleak. The trees had started to shed.

Let me tell you how it was. Random images erupted like hallucinations and I caught myself helpless before a kind of video screen. But this screen was projected from within, onto the back of my skull. I saw us creep toward the pear tree and make off with fruit that belonged to another man; and I heard the word again as I spoke it, well-chosen for its point, that broke the rules of decency and stabbed her in the back, and drove her to weep and from the restaurant; and other events. But whatever the picture, it was unique to the one it was meant for, that is to say, only to me. Interestingly enough, none of these terrible sequences demanded my suicide. For after a thousand years on the meadow of wailing, we, the bodies, moved toward a cleft in the rocks that stood in the east, and departed from the land, cleansed and lighter than the dust, on our final journey. But I am getting ahead of myself. By the second day in the Valley of Eye, we all thought we were going to collapse from boredom and regret but we knew deep down that no, it wasn't like that. The tongue is a slab of metal and it's difficult to move it, and racked by moans, you're trying hard to get your breath. When you do manage to suck in some air, that's really too bad, because it's rancid, and the hallucinations jump up like puppets, to torment you afresh. Plus, I was struggling to keep from touching the heart next to mine — which would have doubled our sorrow — at the very moment I was most in need of contact with bodies. But there

were no bodies, only a heap of discarded clothing on the plain. I had
been expelled from the recurrent nightmare of *egoism*. I had become, in
the words of a poet, "a dull slave grinding at a heavy quern" — and a man
without conviction or friends, or any real plan. In the end, I had strangely
reverted to my phenotype. The answer had been in front of my face all
along. But what then?

o   o   o

One morning I went out into the snow and put some of it in my pockets.
I put it in my shirt, underneath my sweater, and stuck my foot in a drift
up to my shins. I then covered my head with the snow, and like that, with
my hair gone to white, I stood by the bird-bath, I don't know, waiting for
the spring. I ignored the scuffles of my body, the fight I was in, old tin
cans tied to a dog's tail. A fearsome racket. A few winter birds — they
were twits, I think — had been left behind in the trees, and you know how
loud they can get. The birds were restless, jumping from branch to
branch, leaving the maples to regroup in the hedges, and flying back and
forth to the bird-bath in the open space. The sky was clearing up as the
afternoon went along. The sky was closed now for good. I was starting to
shiver, but then one by one, the old self and the dead self climbed from
the pit with Danielle and stood up in front of me. We were two people out
of our heads. Perhaps it was the influence of something I had read that
winter, a seductive nihilism — but even that would have been understand-
able. To have been under an illusion about the mythos, and now clarified.
There's no difference, I said to her. Where had everyone gone to? The
noises had died down in the garden. The fighting had stopped, and I went
with the flow. *Like a legged-legged fly upon the stream.* It's funny to think
about it now, to go over it. Talking to myself in the plural, everyone
solemn but pleased at some remarkable turn of events. We had lost our
nerve; we had all choked, as the expression went. But they were no help
to me, that day out in the snow, no help at all.

The upshot of all this stupidity is that I caught pneumonia and couldn't
get out of bed for over two months. And that's how I confronted the
spring of 19___, flat on my back mumbling in and out of delirium,
noticing that the blossoms had arrived but not remembering when, and
feeling the days lengthen around me but not aware of how much time had
elapsed. I was elsewhere; I was in two places at once — or was it that one

place had become two? I was in bed, and no longer like myself, underneath the surfaces of a pond with tiny one-celled animals floating and multiplying. It was vague, where the animals lived. I hadn't gone very far, but there was a suggestion of terror and also a kind of immunity from it, if only my body would relax below the pond, and keep its eyes and ears opened. If I turned to look elsewhere, then a powerful anxiety would start up — the Greek article *ai,* in the feminine plural, expanded and filled in the foreground of what I saw; and occupying the dark mud composing in the heart of it, the seed of perishing like a mouth, dark dark dark, everything around it was dark, and no ground to stand on and fight.

All of this was part of my delirium. Some of it no doubt came from the books I had read or the television, maybe the bulk of it did. But during this time, I crossed paths with no agreeable images — no Venus on the half-open shell; no table furnished with a bounty of good food and talk; no swimming or dozing at the beach, in the shade of an almond; no victory dances or festivals of the Jonkanoo — nothing of the kind one thinks of as scrumptious — no lovemaking with a big-hipped woman, no apotheosis of the national hero, no flowering poinsettia trees on the slope, in the botanical gardens.

Instead, resembling the works of Max Ernst and Wifredo Lam, I was becoming a shape of shapes: a round demon fading into the canvas like old paint, no longer visible and distinct, or clear and distinct like an idea, not a vermilion feather from a parrot, and not much more than an outline.

I don't know. How much of what I saw happening was in the dream, and how much belonged to the other dreamers, the elders? How much of what I knew and was had been passed on to me?

The languages scrolled in front of my face from top to bottom, poem after poem in un-intelligible sentences with confused punctuation, and in the silence of these words the bull, the forms of hardship spreading from Niger to the shores of the Congo, northward to the Delta, and then west again, to the point of Cadmus' embarkation. I said to the poet of the sentences:

Tell me what I can't tell myself
what lies just out of reach of my tongue.

The city of your speech was before my time, and will be standing still after my time is over. This much I know: what I cannot hope to know. I know this: that before the sun stopped its whistle in the stony legs of Memnon, which told us of the dawn's approach; and before the pale blue fires of hell began to spit, and the gates of delivery were shut — that before these events took place, your poetry was already a hard dwelling upon the earth, the result of migrations long ago. And yet, between the time of its making and my discovery of it, this time is as nothing next to the time to follow — and when I look at it like this, I can't stand it, the city begins to seem fragile and not ancient, but only transitory, and short-lived, like a drop of water on a hot-plate. I hate the thought of this death. Then it was over, and I was well enough to sit with a book in my lap, and to look out at the garden, and even to go outside for a walk, on the warmer days.

In those weeks of my convalescence, the afternoon light hit upon the apples with a breathtaking clarity. My front room was like a chamber flooded with light, tangible, irreducible, and strong; things shifted in it, and acquired a glow, a capacity of depth and thingness, and a color. It was the light as light, stripped of metaphor, something produced by the sun and reaching through the window like a messenger, and the message was — itself. Here I am, the light said. You can talk all you want, but this is how it's going to be. I won't make you rich, and I can't bring back the months you lost, and I won't sweet-talk a girl into your bed. You poets are always asking the light for hand-outs like that. I don't want your incense, or any bulls. Nonetheless, here I am, *poikilothron'*, to be with you for a little while, as long as it lasts. With this language pouring in at the window, I felt calm for the first time in months, more possible or even plausible as a self —

I had visited several cities during this time, and now I could say what they had been: only camels on the horizon of a song, and it took them a whole year to make the crossing. A caravan of cities, each of them with its own courtyard, fountains, and sculpture. These were the cities of my imagination. One day, when I looked up from my book, they had gone.

Jennifer Moxley

ENLIGHTENMENT EVIDENCE
poems for Rosa Luxemburg

red room, it means nothing other than resistance
and remember her back into my living
lost in the dazzling love of you my surroundings
Germany threw her off, and throws the point of present day
you reconnoiter this meager house coat based on a shading
a color of history, my religion nostalgia and this
mood, iconoclast you the practical can seem too firm
headed for neuralgia for christ's sake to be unnerved
means different when Rosa is not dead weight as I have
become for you

———

open field, the privilege to limp across desire
no simple anchorage works when exile is a state of
time past, the wasterly girlhood can call me from
your ways entreating lover and I shall pettily dream as
Rosa limped without a country your solution-less must be
my homeland now since eyeward I befall the open field

———

dissenter is wantonly the name I gave to you
of the paper with the bad intent betwixt impression
and ownership lies idolatry worth every flagstaff
obelisk and needle caressing one million small buds
the forest is damp beneath you legs and embarrassed
work cannot be the volleying of pet names real world man
let sweetness be the creator of moments, building revolution
one kissing at a time

———

January 15, 1919, good-bye Victoria
your mantle of grace and interiors elevated as a faint mist
remove the opus and remains a green wall, that binder of rooms
a twenty-first elopement in issue no small document
to fall in the hands of righters now, without politic
my engagement within is all I know Spartakus
because no one returns my calls to exist, holy shit
I lied about not caring but parallel I insist
as lovers we are bereft by our pairdom
for these domestic settings refuse to let this fairly dated moment
bequest its final death

———

declaration, be it in August or January
confirming each consecutive day of siege the record weakness
grows stronger, is sound relative of the waiting nation
consensus, is this the silence I hear throughout the room,
comrades' testimonies have ended examination, the international
elected thinkers of a heretofore unthought of people
in store for us my bleeding heart
that sound caught in the radio lending
new fear for history now no longer
put off but prevented

———

this polished vehicle, a mid-century wasteland renamed the body
unveiling blamed but influence was the wall that kept things physical
no longer my rebellion
without movement this form too often remembers notice as achievement
what nerve is drenched sentiment, the intellect moved
growing stationary my beloved within your cavernous ear,
use this miracle against me and still I'll claim
your ablest touch remains by rote for all your so-called daring

———

the rumor, it isn't merely a found perception
but the celebration of manly kind
underground living made you monstrous Leo, a forgetter
notorious, evasion always floats above
fucking day to day
supposed hours flourish, they are stone like in memory
while opening words and walks display evaporation
hence the lady's journal, hence the letter entreating
for even I don't remember my overt life anymore
erector though I was, and you quiet hours of dawn
where is your confirmation now except
in everyone else's mouth

———

Tieless make this life, given kindly yet not
wholly, Rosa my hearth burns bright away, a far away
where no gun shoots and like minds tremble
undiscovered until beyond each other's sight.
The printer's place a power a cloud's distance gone
down, find the hiding millions creased in space, the weight
of their quotidian turning earthward in the face
of their familiars, there is no sacrifice worth time
and death I've turned away

———

Where tonight, where when this gut of hesitation
enwraps my small conviction, it breaks out not
but for a comment, a distant day, the chide will will
a fiery speech though your still lit drink shall kill
renewal and the new year waft, it blows cold. I die
to turn askance and never without this constant pulling
memory return, I dedicate to you this gad
for guided we shall never be, our restive footfalls
on an endless threshold

———

what a horror the forever treadable, flip
the dialectic and we are the Freikorps hitting
skulls in the Hotel Eden, exposing weakness
through tiny increments of shifting power
and strength, our imagined finish line
is the end of reason, the irresistible tantalization
of presence, lips pressed together open
to eat and are nourished at the expense
of ideas, but it feels delicious the illicit
taste of you right now, please send me
one hundred flowery lines while you're away
for this resistance is so lonely I shall surely
die of my own righteousness

---

gesture the feminine my way, the aspect subliminal cruelty
what lifeless data will save you
when tedious peace hangs down and our love becomes
ungracious, the mean desires the comfort of a hesitant kiss withheld
I saw this in your face and in all the efforts fatigued
the ineffectual feminine building a life with bold retort,
to bind my bearing witness I will say I speak in mocking
of the foreign news you've brought,
I will veer in subliminal cruelty

---

finer things, the endless derivations of rented rooms
of flowering thought, the change of heart
the watchful eye necessitates, each dissident
moves me Russia and I have broken a rented room, tell me
the wish assaults the will for what it may render
and I'll beat you soundly with unity whims
as yet was my prison unmindful, be good
and you can grow with me
unpunished fearful seriousness,
unclothed in nuance asunder intention
evidence border flux and know
what I have always planned for us
has been by structured futures undone

HOME WORLD

I will say what the register calls forth,
the range of the heart
a journey in the strap of speech,
unrealized, failing to grapple
with even the first word,
or world where I saw humans
in the shadows of buildings
unable to speak at all.
Their dark needs
had grown a weedy tent
over the earth, laid bare.
They could not see
the river for the bank
yet still kept talking
about the bridge.
I lived there too,
saw innocence
among the old
grown willowy.
My illusion could not deflect the float
or the filth upon it,
and all that foliage
what could it have meant
in the light of adornment?
When I remembered nature
as an evil dream
that interrupted my house
and destroyed my family,

leaving me to covet.

I dreamt my sense could wend the fight away

and carnage was my hollow nourishment.

I could have grown tall,

but I awoke to no words and wonder left.

ODE ON THE END

In afterlife
I stood
and wished the depths
of fright
to crumble
by random
weights and measures.
I could not feel
my morals
at the borders
of darkness, I
was left alone
by an unfinished
thought, like a fool.
I found that lack
of place, un-
imaginable after-
math all on
my own. My discovery
so emptied me
a stairwell
into Hell
would have seemed

most welcoming,
a landscape, death red,
the moderate grade
of enemies
gradually accustomed
to anything
the mind
might think. The mere
recognition of it
would be at least
a seed of sense
to wish a future
up from. And yet
to my eye
from this vacant
drape
a better place
appeared, equal measures
of air and earth
came to me
precious enough,
I wore them
well knowing
my thoughts
would think me
hollow, exiled
to the abandoning
company
of all
my illusory
ends.

FIN DE SIÈCLE GO-BETWEENS

There you are in the hinterland chiseling
Nations into the ocean as I await torrential
winds. In our search for beauty we've left
our footprints for the Native informers of narcissism
to uncover once we've fled. We should have let
the out-of-work jesters jingle gun toters
and just gone on with the Eros of coastal waters.
I'll hide your lesser self inside this bird of paradox,
a place dispatchers won't mistake it for any
errant sign of life. While we've been talking
they've lined up along the border towns
heavy with wistfulness, so if ever lip service
might save the planet let's hope it's now,
jettison that charm however and we might be
the end of something gathered.

AFTER FIRST FIGURE

It is illusory
a fitter memory,
a prostrate signifier,
breach / bridge / causeway.

Knowledge lies   shrug
with capacity, got it, everyone
can give birth
and balance between pleasure wavering
(the impression kept) and
the pain of doubt.

This is a future, a coming
that is the ecstasy of non-abandonment.

The sad and fragile admittance
of taken space, is past imagined
pure linear advance
we grab on because we can,
because we are opposable.

Still the shunted
of course, of what is, is sheer sign.
And as with imagination
there is no choice
being thought bound
the separate mind stands out, as matter
and maintains dreamily:
"I have been over to the words and they work."

They are the future
rejecting the read (refinement)
as the attempt to sanity (processed)
"nay"
for no heeding choice is given,
as if the freedom to document
the seemingly dubious lighthouse light
could say more keenly: isolation.

Convenience must admit
exclusion in the rhetorical question
(a signal for logic)
We might lust for others, but never may
obscure meaning
in a claim of taken space.

ODE TO PROTEST

It's as if to be real
you and I must garner backers
without a rib to call our own.
We make ripples
with daily effort and then suddenly
flood the place with anger.
Ours is the anger
of the lowly,
we see life
from the knees up.
What vision we had
on that glorious day,
even the weather
stood aside and let us pass.
But because we could not write
our hearts could not be read,
and when we wrote
it's then we could not publish.
And so a so-called prince
came along and told our story.
He called us "feeble weavers"
ignorant fury
animal instinct
wild in the streets.
If only we had means
then we would give light
to meaning. But for now
it seems royalty will keep writing

the book on right-of-way

and we again shall lay

our lives by the wayside.

THE RIGHT TO REMAIN SILENT

In foregoing witness
against ourselves,
what risk,
this clean towel,
or breakfast
intact by moments.
Fear the state
that could eat many lives
just hanging
on the hope of
divine punishment.
Singing together
we know not who
we serenade,
if not ourselves
who are no selves
and broken
we look to bedtime,
elope with big
distance in mind.
Space is a vicious map
erected by the
trampling of destiny.
If you can only live
one life, you must die
for those
you throw away.

CAST OF SHADOWS

Niggling Spring, the distant palaver
of subjects in the craven bite
of the opening air, in wanders
a holster-wearing mussed Apollo
gushing the beckoning tirade,
bedazzled credo beloved of sports
and the yearly hoax begins.

In a moment good reason will be shunned
for the tinny whistle of the calliope,
the fragile petalled entreaty
of heart's-ease erase a tedious legacy
of schedule, shuffle the mind back
through a violent sequence of mise en scène:
mankind mismated to misery.

Cleaving still to it
humanity a coterie of cruelty
bends over backwards to forget
the sky's no nimble chariot
nor ever will be,
no matter the yearly rebirth
or self-induced labor we cop.

The brass light of day mocks
more readily possibility's hollow
following winter's shut-in drear,
gerrymandered love interests
come knocking down the heart block
demand a lamp granted, hope
and all across the sky, uninterrupted sun.

SPACE REMAINS

What we look into
is space; inside color.

Take color away, space
expands — blue,
unblue.

Ribbons of it unfold,
cause air to sway,
cause the radiance
that should be "bird."

The body is unalone
and reliant for form
on an outer beauty.

ANOTHER, BEING

Quickly —
a quality of leaving — no,
not being, of no "here"

to be within.
But being within itself.

Itself, the utilized force,
to be carried off, and known
for this nonbeing —

no longer anywhere — body —
that which color could be seeking,
at a point unchanging and unreached.

BUT FOR NOW

There is no deciding shape,
image. It moves in, out.
Is there and turning.

How recall the one
only?

I see thousands in a dark sky.
A cloud hovers, an unassimilable
red, within which an object,
moves undetected.

Mind shifts from there
— where dark moves
against dark.

All images are permanent.
What is unreached

by eye, mind —
holds itself.

ANOTHER AND ANOTHER

Comes. Uncolored
because light
exceeds lines
of body.

The body is moving and is not interrupted
by light. Reaching higher, it evades
its own characteristics.
Only light moves in its own
dazzle: hawk.

It climbs and light is again
filtering past the frame of its color.

The bird is a minimal thing
and is not becoming itself.
A light which is total
is touching its body.
The bird passes through
its own resonating
color.

Body and light move, rise,
until one takes the other.

ANOTHER ONE

Came down, down,
and eye following this line —
of flight — as though moving
time itself, yet
only to see.

This looking forward, being poised
on a line
of flight
in terms of vision

leads always to disappearance.
But because sky is also
a remembered feature
there occurs no fact
of emptiness.

VIEW

Distance is held.
The frame retains
promise of
repetition: having,
in mind, image,
in memorized land.
The neck pulled in,
a muscular beat. And a whiteness,
accrued on the horizon, drives,
linearly, into being —

Another time these — numbers, colors,
roam different space.

They are bodies illuminating
area, in mind, and that distance
is thought.

IN THESE PARTICULARS

Our contentment — is defined by acquisition —
of image, color, depth.
Say the distances themselves rise and
disperse as the object approaches —
So the name nears the object, nears itself.
We gain, gain
the bodies light would disperse.
And each name amasses its particulars.
Here is the mode of brown on one foot.
Here is what foot is not.
Here are the wide mammalian eyes.

The moment that fails is past. Body enters
the future at a comfortable amble.
Didn't you say we were surrounded —
that sound and light adhered to these forms —

that the ocean — great gash — was a solution
of sorts — didn't we need
to look there also desire being
a form of motion
past the frame of body — also of blindness —

The object, then, leads us inevitably
past itself. Its name, disjoined.
Our futures in the smallest, mute curve.

FEATHERS

Even when motionless
body resists
viewing "as a whole."
Color and line — whiteness
and the whiteness of memory

blend and re-begin.
We look — an object
traced in its entirety
against an area of
nullification.
Against the stone
of nothing being blue.
Against the stone of
nothing animate.
The possibility of
flight is told in present
stillness.
The body, as a whole,
exists only as abstraction.

These moments, *feathers*
only to be.

PATTERNS OF IDENTIFICATION

Look — nothing falls.
Light is captureable.

A consciousness of body
permits vision of another.

These curves are curves
of intention.
Movement is checked.
So, there is a consciousness,
of disbelief — each beat,
wings
re-enter a world.
Each length —
measured against
nonbeing.

FRAME BY FRAME

Body gains height, speed,
vision.
Then, cessation, rest.
Change is totalizing
but forms no composite.

In time, a series of portraits
appears, and that accumulation
supplies full sequence —
and what is not.

This body is abrupt.
Its change (of direction,
aspect) proves space
unfillable.

TO WITNESS TO HUNT

Recognition of the object
is a recognition of body —
self being apart
from
holding posture.

It waits — body,
object.
It is sitting at the highest point,
for view.
It is sitting — and blue also sits,
a component.
These last and move.
The turning of the head
reveals another feature,
of greatness.
And body holds these in wind.
Against wind's demand of
bodilessness — as enforces
movement,
impermanence — the way
the whole

hungers

HERE AND THERE

Color — idiosyncracies
of movement —
follow descriptive
language.

I see
that the object corresponds
to amassed knowledge.

We search
sky for
words of flight

animal — here —
and in the abstract

SURROGATE HOUSES

1.

The candle of watching

                    it all melt.

Angled hands of
the clock circling

a kitchen wall.

                    You have your secrets

poured into syrup onto circles.

Does it start in the eyes   the ears?
          It's a section

of cycles   we're pooling our portions.

                    Tension's tinny motive to locate. Action   value.

It's a click   it's done   it's undone   it's a loud cord

according to attitude   longitude   device.

2.

Above the sky is another layer of sky.

            A matter of perception

the side that sags.

                In the idling aisles of merchandise we respond

to the vivid labels   the suggested servings.

Blowing up objects to see how they fly

apart.

            Can the pilot cry?
            Can you switch chairs?

                    When we remember it is remarkable we are breathing.

This black candor flooding the sun each puddle

little   canned   floating your image back   crying iron.

3.

Colored by comparison   an invisible

placard of culture.
The viable other.

Tracking our hands across a window

making faces at absence   what is familar is strange   exciting

          everything being everything.

                    We aim for smooth

surfaces to place a glass of water

and it is seconds   sweeping a corner

to stand on   our need for signals   describers

scribes   cries of what you never had and knowing that

4.

If we wake up saying I'm thirsty

who will bring us water?   Will the walls hold?

    Weather becomes mechanical when love dismantles

        possession in conversation.

How has been a long while

you can keep this.

           We know where we have

us steady
hardening the surface   building buildings

      to sleep. The chapel bells clap twelve.

You seek   stung by the sun   your solar

plexus flexed   breathing   composed for a blow.

5·

Noon is to be rested in the city   tired of talking.

        A pillow blocking the eyes   strains

of imagined music
ghosting to the time

you keep   squinting wishes.   It's running away.

We see faces

        the features we can kiss.

Skeleton of a burnt church on Gough.

            But sleep peels our eyes open   it is dreaming

in a different city   no more blank film. A cubicle

a newsstand   the produce.   Open bars crowding.

6.

You contemplate
        rejoicing in thick strands

of hair.   A full cylinder.

        Characteristic heritage.

To sweep up these loose ends
        undo this given

we string meaning along a sentence.

                Seventeen years

ago meant cold cuts and juice. There is forgiving

                fathers. Ground   ground up   sky then.

The sense
we speak for others.   Your mother running

in velvet pants. The crumbled story

you stumble towards   with a mending flag.

SHRED

we are complicating
patterns. destiny

      is a big room. we talk
like jets missing

home: a view of sky as a child.
a cotton diorama.

birds collect where they will.
telephone wire. the front stoop.

what days aren't pinched by absence

we are here
in our skin. destiny

      is a small city.
I could die today.

WALK*

Longing tags along. Shadows. She walks
Through doorways. False assumptions swell equally real.
So get drunk one night. 5 bucks for the bartender
To kiss her on the mouth. Slipping him the tongue.
Letters in the small desk drawer. The creases deepen
And get out of my head, she thinks. Inked words
Soften like memory or the voice that spoke
Right in her ear. It stains the wood darker.
His leg favoring walk did her in.
Both swagger and vulnerability.

---

*"Walk," "Answer," and "Play" are drawn from a sonnet series entitled
Distance Times Time Equals Velocity.

His kindness comes to her just like that
Limping. To know the oceans separate.
He experiences her city's fog
On the football game. She's somewhere under it.

ANSWER

To call and find no answer leads her
To suspicion. Love described as fire.
She misses foliage dying in color.
Reminds her of falling. A trust in dead leaves.
Wind is an absence. He wanted to hear
The line over & over. A permanence
In telling. She describes everything.
A cup of coffee. Burning the old bed
On the beach. It does not make location
Any more real. There is no metaphor.
That second delay between their voices.
She wonders about the connection.
Hesitant to question. The only answer
He can give her is that he has none.

PLAY

Don't play me. If a kiss at midnight
Insures. Toasting themselves and a ball drops.
Fuck that. Reshape the self to fit into
The life of another. An empty bottle
Rattles. How scary the thought is. Actually.
If they met half-way it would be Kansas.
The watch from the pawn shop. He gave it to her.
Worry the pen's tip thinking of his leanness.
A wrestler. Dull ink full of mouth. She
Says the opposite of what she really means.
The outline of scars felt in the dark.
Pedaling through the park & yelling at the ocean.
A repetition of tenses.
And she plays that song over again.

BARE
for Tom Clark

A gap like industry betweeen us,
Patched with histories. You had your business
That trick of the unfinished address
As though the doorway behind us were liquid,
A randomness, a darkness of one's own.
We say, "Have a good day", but mostly we look
Of speech. A story worn out from telling
That passes in an airplane of words
For months. Suddenly you're carrying yourself
To the ruins of the bathhouse that make our
Structure exposed. Here. There. Solitude is
And I can almost hear that. I am sure,
Peer over the sharp edge. The crumbling as when
Jimmy describes the sun. It goes. It goes.

HERE
for K. H.

I took the same train the others took,
Spread out and unknown at least. You fight snow;
Holding the night awake, troubled to need
An audience, so dry, that game of chance.
Things come out which were not things before
Shaken from my sure boot. To my friend
I would say, if she listened, dancing
Audibly against the oncoming weather,
The carnival quickens! The noisy damned!
There is more to a lover's suicide
Than fits on a postcard, hope all is
Well. The long path of lead unflattens,
Passes cities broken under bridges:
We roll that way, look for a calming fact.

Mark Nowak

Stworzenie

You must not whisper these words in the darkness. These words
these. You must not whisper them.

So began the world. In the darkness
so began the world. The world began this way. It began with these words.

You must not you musn't no.

The gods they said do anything but don't do that. Said that to kids just born.
They knew they would. Said you must not you musn't no and knew they would.

What a way for gods to start the world.

Would think they could do better than that. Would think they could forgive.

But they didn't, and these words these
nobody wants you to know.

Zwiastowanie

"I am a goat browsing in the corn."
"I am St. Casimir blessing owls in the trees."

(We speak of identity w/ split tongues . . .

"I am fertilizer pouring from a wound in my side."
"I am sewing sheep-costumes for the wolves."

"I am St. Casimir cooking fish on a kerosene stove. "

"I am wearing a bird-skin parka."
"I am St. Casimir in black wooden shoes."

"I am the head of a goat on the street-lamp in front of your house."

(Even the saints forget themselves . . .

"I am from the village of Gorzen Dolny."
"I am the hornets' nest in your left ear."

"I am St. Casimir, goddamnit. Look at these goat-skin shoes."

(Listen, freak, tell me who you are . . .

"I am the corn and nothing but the corn. So help me god."

"I am the mile you walked back to your name."

The sun rises each morning simply because I am separated from the sun.
                    If there were a way for me to
tie a string to it, ride its path at a comfortable distance from its rays,

then I might not need to enter my house in the morning.
then I might never have to leave my house again.

To reach Pittsburgh by six o'clock in the morning, *droga,* the sun doesn't plan.
Nor does it project to arrive in the Pacific Northwest around six a.m.

Dawn, like sound, is evanescent. It is like a struck gong that is going
out of existence. It disappears itself into the light of my morning.

If there was just a story for this, a young girl who slept so long she finally went
blind, and in her complete night she was able to tell us how the sun won't rise,

how it's we who step from our sleep to notice it again.

"An American is a complex of occasions."
                                        – Charles Olson

The house or hand that forces an American into you.

The approaching arms the approaching horizon arrive.

The approaching horizon that opens out over the prairie.

Arrives at the house and forces open the door.

He would open the door for the equivalent of a dollar.

George Washington lived without ever opening the door.

The hand that signed the Declaration of Independence.

The house at which the approaching horizon arrives.

Henry David Thoreau never visited the prairie.

He arrives at his house and imagines opening the door.

Approaching arms the book he wrote before you.

Before you, *grób,* Thoreau and Washington arrive.

Arrive with arms that are pointed toward the prairie.

Arrive with arms that forced you open before.

How shall I praise you, polis, as the center or
the snare at the center.
Either of you is not an eye, is why
so often you are
at the mouth of a river. You are a saying,
polis, and a devouring.

Or so it got put by one *teoria,* which has little
to do with diamonds or the southwest side of
Chicago.
But perhaps a bit, for when we
go there, we go there to stay,
by which we mean simply that it is a good
place to have sausages.

I wonder if Wittgenstein ate sausages.

To beg the question, how shall I praise you, what
can I say about you
that you don't proclaim
on your own. You are a gatherer of bodies, of
the very youngest and the very oldest of bodies,

which you devour. But what about Heidegger,

does he eat sausages? So you are a mouth, poetry
has found a way to you, but already you're off
propagandizing,
aware
of the correct pronunciation of "welcome" in
forty-seven languages.

But did you know, *teoria,* did you know, polis,

that there are tongues that refuse your words,

there are mouths and gums, lips,
in which to say welcome means "what has
gone wrong
for you?"

We have by now observed that the practice of agriculture
        could explain certain things,
    the notion that we can transfer guilt & suffering is
        familiar to our spirit.
Yet when it arises between the materials: scythes, barley,
    stones . . . it is then that the world
Acts, from our refinements & theology, to bear upon
        the castoffs
    we see as falling to Hell, us all.

And birds, they with their din expand the field, whose cheep
Does rid their need of *sprawdzic*. To them their gods
They are the winds, the castoffs from Heaven.
"They are the owl (of ill omen) that hoots in the town."
And that it is the world who sets the boundaries for them,
        for they

Would wish the world instead to give rise, and the thunders
        surge
Across the farmhouse. They adore those gardens, over
The gate, through a hole in the fence always made just for them.
Beside the creek the owl sets its claws upon two snakes.
That brought rain, brought by an access to wind.

These (Terra, Aqua, Ignis, Aer) could not mimic the world, the wife
With child, the farmer smiles at a storm gathering, he looks up
And believes the same befalls his in-laws,
Believes this to be more than a local occurrence: it is this daze
        that traces on the heels of humanity.

The calendar of you, *zboze*, yield of Demeter, and the moon, the north star, these also are songs.

    When it is understood that to renew the objects

(a hawk, bluebirds, a bear . . .

these narratives used by the one who seeks are supposed to have songs of their own.

    I would suppose, *zboze*, that the house the plow broke the prairie for had not these hymns at heart; and yet the grass is pregnant with you.

The calendar, the yield of Demeter, the moon and the north star. A hawk, bluebirds, and a bear.

    I learn the prairie not by the mouthing of these names, nor any others. Not even the songs I've learned will save me here.

Nebraska, a tune my throat caught. Iowa, a drum that nobody's tuned.

Minnesota, a river so dark that even the fires won't touch it.

The winter is gathered, as are we, and only the first foot of you, *zboze*, is still left standing on this earth.

    And then the snows come to cover you.
    And then the earth is laid upon our graves.
    And time, it is still the origin of time.

(Grzech Pierworodny . . .

A painting of the Garden of Eden
(found in Kolaczyce, Poland . . .
          in which everything is red.
The apples,
The tongue of a jackal,
A rooster's plume.
                    Even the rooster's
legs are red, the rooster's feet
    & the jackal's tongue
is poised next to Adam's left leg.

One unicorn, one snail,
          one snake is winding up
the apple tree with apples
                    (they are only
half red . . .
          Adam's tongue, in his
red mouth: red. Eve's tongue is red.

    Three hills behind two chalices.
    One shovel that I think is a tree.

              But who this father
that didn't want us
to know, Who made taking
what's red
          (become . . .
awareness, difference, & banishment
in our very first story?

So much for red. So much
for having red.

Off-shore,
even if there was
a shore,
          some
distance from it.

To forget
what comes next,
odzew,
          what
the wind sweeps
across the water,

even if there was.

To give name to what
we cannot grasp
theoretically.

What we cannot grasp,

believe it or not, we cannot
lay hold
of all things

and make them theorems.

                    So you are
surprised, *odzew,*
casting out below the bridge
     where the river empties
to the bay,

even if there was
a bridge or river.

"There was a river"
you whisper to a child,
except, except . . .

Things happened,
unnameable things
happened.
            The fish, well,
there were fish in the river.

Now there are none.

            There was
a beauty in the way this
river was described
by the townspeople, who were,
by and large,
dependent upon the river.

But now?

Now it is forbidden
to even mention the former
tributaries of this river.

Of course,
Of course in the out-buildings
(and behind the fire-house)
has spread a mythology,
            which has grown,
grown in relation to
the disappearance of the river,

so that now, why,
one would almost think
that it still flowed
out into the bay.

One might still be deceived
into believing,
    yes, believing that a boy
could walk the dirt road
out of town

and return
(as evening settled upon
the elms and porches

with a basket of fish.

But if this did, in fact,
happen.
    If a boy walked
down the dirt road and
over the bridge
with a basket of fish,

what would we say?

Would we believe, *odzew*,
that the time had returned
for music and dancing?

    Or would we
assume the boy a thief,
jail him,

and continue to interpret
our mythology?

In the northern range in the mountains, "neighborhood" it is called
their starting place.
                          Often the sun rises very red the sun crosses
the horizon. At harvest time the corn like the women and men
                          return
to their houses. As the dry ears are laid to be stored
through the season when the fields lie barren,
                                                this is the time
                                                this is the evidence
of the time when one travels to the cemeteries and addresses
the Lord of the Dead.
                          And the contrast of this life of ours on this earth,
krzyzowanie,
the surface of this earth in contrast to the Underworld to the sky.

Without the earth for him or her to walk across, the day, year . . .
                          returns (even in
                          these mountains)
the dimensions of the house to the cyclical paths of the sun.

Heather Ramsdell

WHERE THINGS OF A KIND

In pause, in
decent pause with plausible
care, to push the matter aside

where were we, intentional
streak on glass, we were aware

of our own breathing, meaning
flows from it, uncomfortable

laughter finds a spare
seat in the aisle, the structure,
seen from above, a grid
we cannot stand outside, allows, as

long as the axes hold true, not blow around,
as long as winds don't come, and
we are meant, not error bending, though a bent

hair on a white
tile is also true, because

isn't the idea
to have it
lifelike. Just the other day I

lost my place.
From here on let's leave crumbs, let us
feel free to walk around.

There are fields.
That line looks like a bridge.
A barge a ground, is

that a fire to your left, the trees
stop, bear with us, that
rock is that
hard, there is no need for proof

now, do not
move. Do not anything.

BRIGHT RECEDING

With speed the prior body
of the tree could not have foreseen

in orange flakes rising from safety
of, this its release from,
the locus of fire into mossy night,

an imaginary fire in actual night.
Amongst blacknesses, that star already
imploded now is the size of

a rose window, actually
I made that fact up. The sun
came through the window again

by such light, some
burnt trees — such
trees in the yard *make sense*

having incongruities which
occlude both, dread numbs
both — both
include part-answers.
And no research gels.

In being numbers, the shadow faces
turn, locate
one end first, one part, color

of orange and red and black, black
as the black of an eye, please
find me my coat, it says.

It says, you cannot prefer both
the image and itself, you cannot reside
in the possible, henceforth,
resolving to climb inside the solid mound, not see.

BRIDGE SEGMENT

.1

> No bridge is wanted, we now see,
> and bridging is the wrong figure.
> — W. V. Quine

From abutment from
abutment, in a series of angled turns
the path of the circle goes awry.

I keep finding my half on the doorsteps there
where the path, if it is a path, without
formal grip of perspective, too abruptly
arrives. As in the step from a subway.
A plane. In gaudy emergence, want

for a hole through which to go — it's cold
outside — and an eye, an eye and, when it is dark,
any light. Any way to build a way to navigate
to, for the scheme of
the sequence not of footfall not of running fore-
to-aft, a splicing as in a film, in a string's
acquaintedness — of the ones
to the other ones, for a tryst when we are tired.

It is simple and we are tired

and the plan is clear but a clock
ticking throughout, some
aging occurs, an attrition cannot
be stayed. The fine
progression of cracks.
Dumb sleep is lost

in trajectory. In the instance
of moveable parts, x misses y
in countless versions of the episode by fractions, plotted
within the blunt dark, by sextant and ship's lamp.

There won't be the closure of books and hands
laid on the table. There was no speeding drum,
not a flag, not a map. It has no legend, and its keys,
I assume, are in the river. There is no bottom.
There is no perimeter, there is nothing if not surface
baldness and its continuous arrangement

which is, exactly, the field.

To call it a prison was mean of them.

Outside, there is no center, between
the dark ground, the dark sky,
at the line difference was no wall
to escape, having already left everything
behind but the task of lunging quickly
toward, where else
is there to go, remember

the stillness of the arc traced
by the falling away of the bodies
which cannot be followed
on foot. They were not just figures.

.2

Then and then a line began but an arrow ensued as drawn without ends

whilst once in the event, before the book fell

during winter, at the same time as morning broke and henceforth

the only apt moment passing in orderly parade a dot

and and delay

the day after that, a delay, at an instant when she was young, the instance,
    suddenly, suddenly, thus

flags of the parted curtain

for the moment, taut with emergency; at a juncture in slow motion,
    formerly these days, often June between the hours of 9 and 2 at ages
    25 through 61, in 1993, a light-year, as they waited the day before
    yesterday when the phone rings, a season ago

ago, when the satellite finally lost its gravity late last week in an eventual

of horizon unmodulated by moment

vanishing dot at a subsequent

over end yet-to-land, to an interval, already hours eons later, one calm
    second, an epoch sunset lapsing in perpetuity if, after the last of the
    future in a minute on a Thursday as the day is long, for the past.

.2

Did I say Thursday? I meant June,
how odd.

A tooth
in a glass
of milk,

a missing
tooth.

·3

A book is on a ledge, its message may not be delivered
intact, on time, or arrives wearing knowledge as wig or badge.

The typographer said a missing dot
in the pattern of dots was sad

as when a subject who impersonated the king
was banished beginning the problem of twos

not to suggest an unbroken pattern as paradise

leading to problems of many, none of them
attached, causing impotence, or seamlessly
configured, causing impotence.

Arrival's scrim is painted so.

With a loupe you may see the small elements – points

where communion breaks, the crazing, the leakage,
gaps, where waste is the platform from which to leap –

keep falling through the mesh. Dear Charles,

I'm fine though not myself
I have but three things to say

in all honesty and alarm the book is on a ledge, it speaks
only of losses in margins, I can't
remember the rest. I'm sorry

there's nobody here by that name.

·4

The door, the door's calm
summary slam. I've forgotten,
if I had ever known, the name for it.
There is grace

in the indivisible brick, and gravity.

Agree, the obvious nerve
strands bunched
cloth against the other
nerves is pressure and
a warmth, not love

exactly — a break in the surface, a lip — a lip

had little to do with the problem of the mouth, not the mashing of a
mouth against that mouth because we were glad and bored that day,
having already slept and eaten, plenty of water, sandwiches, milk and figs
had entered the mouth, living bloods of the body within, small breath in
and emitting from the mouth, strings of saliva and, things we found
unthinkable eventually scorched through the mouth, an effusion, a dry
wind through the slender tube opened a flame in the mouth igniting,

you, it said

you, and a pattern emerged,

in the body, she is thinking

of a word. I am thinking of a word, you,
in the last row, nod, if you can hear me.

·5

Snow covers the tracks we left, the dogs
couldn't follow from, past the naked trees,
the slopes had little grip we had to run
quickly and with an expression of certainty
into the field, although

there is no clear route, through this field
the way must be made up
while going along there is a sense
of being

near the river blurred
with ice. The sun

is white. The land,
blind by it, the sky is

snow and horizon
impossible. It is impossible

from this far station in the rows
to tell much

of fault. Of who they are but people
some small distance apart, one

chasing, one running
away, when time,

over the flat ice budged, when

all the sound went out,
still running.

The screen goes black

in the tradition of sleep, one
falls, one would first, night

amongst the animals in act
of matter's stark need for fuel

a twig for heat a morsel
on the bone I love you.

We should have been home by now.

.6

I'm told the life of the fire was brief
though productive. Soon the fog of ashes
will soften and cover this too.
In the manner of ash, not to be sorted
then restored. Of course this
is the province, however encrusted
in scaffolds, who can say if the boards
are sound —

the water is potable, the air improved,
but the street has no direction,
the street is littered with vacant gloves
figures, the trees
won't bear resemblance
not a leaf, no further need of sirens

          — whether the bridge was
saved if this place is the right the
same or a viable one or was ever
ours to have failed, to be pardoned for.

I am a tourist. Amongst the indigenous
tourists, unable to offer directions,
motion in the street is inching
steadily toward or away, a clock
ticking throughout. An exit an arrow
at every turn a clock, some aging occurs.

We noticed the passing facades, stacked
of foils and formica, of stonework
and ash, how they hung from the sky
as a sham for the unseemly wards

and cannot be cheered. This is not
what the book said.

Eventually into the angled streets, we called
wherever we ended up most frequently
our homes, returning the same
half-open eyes and lopped mouth.

·7

You must wear your identification to be
admitted *in the building at all times*
to be seen to belong, without regard
for the referent face, a sense of figure discerned
as by surveillance, the shutter's malfunction
just as the vital face of *x* upturned.

Who applied to represent themselves?

In an unfair light we are moving
with nauseating speed, either the background
blurs or we blur but the room is a real
room with its attendant rug and door, a series
of arrangement, the random accretions.

A chair has no assignment We
are also composed.
                    If the clock stopped
the clock wouldn't care. If we're not
the ones we claimed we are — the small
yellowing wouldn't be helped — I am sure
I am real and the others. Our matter
is tolerant, but only prepared
for such blights as have already been imagined.

And the strength of the thread
does not reside in — this isn't the yellow
the fact that some one fibre runs — this
yellow is not realistic, it wants
— *through its whole length, but in*
the overlapping of many fibres. Memory

coaxed from odd threads of the subsequent found
on a historian's lapel in a sterile bag on a rack of like bags.

Who was last to leave, which one drew
the curtain aside, did the couple,
heard laughing in the room above run, where
was the she last seen, did the hand?

What did the hand?

Who was really the last to leave? The lights
stayed on, the films grew very clear.

.8

Some agreed to trade their grief for a larger one.

A carrot grows
tiresome, a misery flies
out by moments.

It becomes possible to attend
the banquet wearing char-clothes and be mere,
the one near the door, of an ilk in a room of others.

A stain as large as the shirt would go unquestioned.

Sufficiencies, shouts, base laughter arise
with the same uncivilized grace of a fox,
run, laughing away with the bird.
When the profound finally comes
to surface it refers to little trips
to the store for milk with modesty
as of milk, inch-meal, a lightbulb is
exchanged for light meaning the light
at the edge of a table says the same
amount as a face/as the sound of a kicked
shard in the street/as a sentence. The verso
of a violin, having lost its front is sold
for five dollars and fifty cents denoting
a music composed as an instrument to hurl
at passers-by, a song called Please which goes if
if and thus thus, and sings, The Masters sing
there is no act but music, all good, and
free wine for everyone, free laughter
from the floor above, footsteps
of excited preparation, nights, days, elsewhere
the custom is drinks for an hour, fights
for an hour, tears for an hour, elsewhere
only tears, or the custom is tea
without comment, a common laugh
seems at first to delay the memorial
service, then trucks go over steel
palettes in the street, an air conditioner
stops then stops relieving us
of the future, Please do not
force the evidence, we'll respond
to no questions beginning with *I*, why
all the resuscitation, the long faces
and decline, let go of this. The end

note resonates until the song
gets taken up again, a dirge,

.9

A curtain
left open, the curtain
is open, no

circle discovered in dust-free conditions
or circular mirror in which
to collect the face by piece

that one eventual shard would
drive sense through all the prior

ends, an arc, for a time, that arm
goes casting out toward

as a body in motion tends toward

a certain point, the possible dividing
itself from the case.

As river; the river.

Frankness is in its brown
surface, radiant
waves where the stone went

extend to the far edge of
leaving

clarity's fine dream of
crashing into a wall.

.9A

Heartlessly so the heart
itself is bloodless, a pocket

things are folded in, noumena protrude
there as a sock might from a drawer

there a choice to own
the gross bluntnesses of matter, rain

tonight on the precipice,
lamp, you cannot be kind.

Pam Rehm

IN ANOTHER PLACE

A keen living doubted my behavior;
navigating without hands or brains, silent
in the depths of the night.

Why can't I ever say believed itself in the center?

The sky is our walk constantly
around the earth. Likewise, motionless
to whatever god there was a temple.
I approached the steps with only arms. Extended.

As we know, straight lines could be arcs of
great circles. To be found if lights
are provided.

In a round about expression, you realize
what we mean, not held any longer. It
would help though. I have May in a
sleeping sickness, repeating dreams with a
regular pattern of sixteen inch round holes.
No voice as the images pass. A bit of
dark sky is seen removed from such haziness.

Normally, impulses move in one direction.
Perhaps you have noted how little thinking
is done. In the length of a dream. When
asked, I see plant growth. Many farmers
and gardeners plant things.

In another place, the air is of greater
density to mirages seen. The sand expands
and cold currents of air pass for some
distance down flowing.

You depend on the weather overhead all day.
Later, in the night, writing any statement you
make a certain condition of the sky more of a
scene. As in advance, predictions can be made.

You looked confused with the word relativism.

This is no common error. Of course, the
flooding makes one act like a mirror. Without
mathematics there is much misunderstanding as
to how our matter stands, on some notion of
what it is all about.

Often, the writer of a story had the hero
fall across the sky. One evening a woman says
she saw a comet. Of course she did not know
where she was looking. What points of a compass
could have directed any conclusion or explanation?

At twilight what is actually happening questions
the beautiful colors of the sunrise.

Sometimes with curtains houses stand. And here,
the objects exist concretely in waiting.
And because there is no today or last our words
hold us fast in speech or else the hand.

Everything is still helpless. The story-teller
listening, he can no longer tell a story but
resides considering the emptiness corresponding
about the things in the mind.

The silence of animals, the seasons move in
silence. My body has become so attached. The
indication gives warning and the distance in its
totality. Why, at this moment bound up with my
organism, I fail just as the child is led
by the mother.

Man can be what he looks like. The wings of
a butterfly are never so clear as in summer.
A boat travels over the lake to make the bird song
a hiding place.

I could confine myself and disappear. I could.
It is true that for a moment the noise of man
is frightening.

A MAN SETS SAIL WITH THE FAIR WIND OF HOPE

Thus we must remind ourselves
of rapture
The line that is here
or bygone
The room, healed
The soup left

Found a route
alongside my excursion
Trapped against a
destination

Rest in one mood
Seated in traveling clothes
Alone
To wander out
To creep into thoughts

No longer does wine lift his heart. Since he never
started he can always stop. Hence, when he says "I
do not," it begins with nothing to do.

Who has particular hours lived for eternity?
And which ones love the accidental?

When all secrets come together he is living in ambush.
To see things again. A spider is a great amusement for
one bored with his native land. Every single change.
Indulged in the hope of an endless journey. Or trip.
Least of all the pilot. His own ship.

* * *

Thus we are reminded
of capture
The pirate who is restless
and pacing
The moon, overhead
The fish, troubled

Sound a song
fit for a stranger
Speech interwoven with
Confrontation

Another world but
to our own
Home which declares itself
Home even in the mist

From this moment on he has only one thing against him.
The water, changes. To a certain degree one must consider
everything in his life a wager. Perhaps he is
often fooled. Looses his masculinity. He recoils on
it knowing how to sink down and hide. That is the motive
for his aimless imagination. He is not a child. It
seems to me he seldom moves.

* * *

Thus we are stirred by
Foreshadowings
A cat that is black
crossing us
The ladder, angle
An umbrella, opened

Walked to feel
a different breathing
Found a way
to continue

Travel
To define nothing
To whom can one turn
To whom is there a constant
position

Now the various squalls have receded. The quiet
activity of forgetting. Tomorrow he is going in such a
way that the remnants of memory will prove to him that
he is still young. Listening to a joke that cancels
the fear of immanent thinking. When sensuousness
appears he cannot find it on any map. Even the legend
is no longer developed. No special piano or porcelain
dishes. Artificial puzzle. Trying to put together
what belongs together. The sailor's yarn, the flag,
the deck; always a welcome quest. To be partially
possessed.

                              *   *   *

So we are reminded
of the cadence
Sinking away into
stillness
An absolute cessation

It is perhaps
that he has never grown
into the present

but the preordainment
imparted to him
was something –
As he looks back on
his past –
apart from his own
power

It is the one being.
It is the one who could almost be himself.
A man sets sail with the fair wind of hope.
A man sets sail when everything in him tightens.
When the land forces its way through him.
He speaks something. The lips come apart to repeat
"the first time." And then, as if rediscovering
his thought, "it is, indeed, despair."

A TRIVIAL PURSUIT

A wonder the scene
is Psyche

Not knowing knowing
to see

Becoming lovers
before there were arrows

There was an Eros
prior to awakening

Thus, crucified into affection
My Eros is curious
in the dark

Wrought with primal force,
the source of trembling

The wound, the mother-lode
of all figure and fable

The children are hidden
from the table

We are all changelings
evoking ourselves

II

Desire for the possession of happiness

Apprehension of an all-embracing
Attraction

Half-way between interaction
Images of images

Oh my right hand
what am I to do

Let the whole house crash
from mood to mood?

Passion moves
lacking in foresight
with a joy all its own

I heard a person saying
Hide this from me

But where can we hide
to escape life's chorus?

III

One cannot avoid impressions
The pressure suggesting a system
of surrender

to attachment or self-confession

A superstitious regard for salvation
and the soul

Each year forever
a fury

To have ten-thousand words
Stained

You are bound to lose your tongue

Hiding from yourself
the things you fear
will mean something

IV

Shadows of images
Images in reflection

Implied is the memory,
all embracing

Possessed by guilt
and its preservation

My Eros is curious
for explanation

The heart a fire

Trembling in the dark

A figure moves
in and out of

THE HUMILIATION OF THE VALLEY

I.

The compass of the moment
reveals an angle of suspense
Doubtful hope or bliss to come
are the only presentiments
pressed heavy in the air
of circumspect

Scarcely do we venture
to admit patience
without prospect
but depict ourselves under
an unspeakable oppression
Cold and peculiar
Independent and somewhat suspicious

Days are passed enacted
And there is no end
come to, to note them

II.

Nowhere a center and everywhere
a periphery

Until you're wounded in a single spot
Permanently without recovery
no impression is made

When conscience is mortalized
you submit to its governance
The only saving grace
is to release the adder
feeding in the breast, unceasingly

III.

Never betray what is received
An undying elemental stream

The imagination forges
an endless penetration
an unquestionable possession
that escapes you through the air
of the centuries

Beguiling the tedium of the way
like an instrument blown
out of scale

What name is on the lips
and in my flesh?
You leave yourself again and again
The tone is infinite
Presence the forever unanswered question

IV.

Ambivalence is seldom a stimulus
It retains a sentiment of protection

Acquainted with few acquaintances
you beg of yourself amusement
In a paroxysm of dialects
To evince a base spirit
To discern a voice within you

What is this leading to?

To recipient, known —
You must follow
an evolution out of
dead notions
Feed on nutrients not notoriety
nonetheless piety
For your only possession
is being possessed

Furthermore, there is trial
in commitment
You'd be witless without it
and much too deliberate

NOVEMBER TESTAMENT

Always a coward
I play the bully

Then beg you
to forgive me

I know it is absurd

When the night cometh
in the silence before dawn

But how shall I look for you,
my soul
I cannot tell time

to stop
I have lost so much
by refusal

A strange reciprocity
once leveled us

Now I can't explain

The empty window
within sight

Cut short of light
the cold has entered

I toss the leaves
and go back in

**

Do you know this fugue
It keeps going round
in my head

Like persistent rage

I cannot escape
Impelling it

Pray,
teach me a better craft
than dependence

**

In one drawer we save
From another we spend

It is one and the same

We are without relations
We have become partitions

We eat from a table
of exclusion

We hear noises
as if they were *meant* for us

We are already burying our children

**

The pauper is equally
our impoverished witnessing

A sign
of our ridiculous lives
on this bank of the river

"What depends on us"
is not "all" or "nothing"

If I nourish myself
If I am sufficient to myself

Who am I then,

Enough?

How often do we touch
our learning?

Paper money
and men's perceptions

What is a profit
and how will it redeem us?

Our hands remain useless

Private

Manipulated
has a man in it

A human centeredness
Where nothing else can enter
Let alone survive

Elio Schneeman

JULY

Abandon these flowers of speech
under the microscope tongues

Indispensable twilight hours

An unwelcome air conditioner
drips mysteriously
                    into the night

Rise, above the humid forest
where the city breathes again

Open fire hydrants gush
onto wide avenues

The parks are open,
movie theatres full

Exquisite nightfall descends
like a welcome kiss

                    *

Under ravaged stars,
a full moon
                    wheels into place

Colored verbs take shape
in the theatre of the skull

Where voices walk freely,
mimicking you in pantomine

Under a cloud cover,
liquid nations wake up

I've abandoned my former vices.
Now sit here, drinking
                              wretched tea

                    *

Lightning songs
quicken the heart,

Summer turns
inside the stomach

What to do
with thunder
                    inside the head?

                    *

Dead spirits
speak to me
                    in foreign tongues

I go out for a walk,
into heavy purple air

Inside the poem,
my old room
                    changes color

Quickens changes
in the heart

Like the sky, l dress
in blue and white

                    *

Daylight breaks through
dreams' rhythm

Where I walk on a bed
of broken glass

Put on the sky outfit
and ride my bike to work

I remember
all my friends

Sucked up into
the vapor I breathe.

*

You wait in the morning
for the sun to rise

It does, like a spread
of orange marmalade

My cat won't eat,
his eyes glazed with heat.

This body like rusty machinery
clinks into place.

*

Cooler today, the wind
blows my thoughts
                    into tropical air

Pigeons make peace
in the skyline of your hair

Outside, the jackhammer
of the city maneuver

Into grooves in your head
with kettle-drum insistence

I close my eyes,
the burning landscape remains.

                    *

I ride through
the evening clouds

Where God plays his concerto
in a mottled mood

Along the tarred rooftops

Thin pools of blood
and anxious hymns reverberate

Cool with desire,
the leaves multiply.

                    *

Night gets old
like a tired dancer.

Lover guide me
into the firmament
                            of the dawn

And protect my shadow
on the darkening lawn.

                    *

I feel depleted, as though
in a thousand stars

The lights put out
in every one

Guns and siren wails
pierce the New York night

Where I wake up
bathed in the vulgarity

Of my dreams,
soothing as an elixir.

*

Dollar bills float
in the scented air

The ice cream truck rolls by
in the summer night

And Medusa raises her head
above the tree line,

Attuned to the clouds.

IN THE VALLEY

Moving in and out of red air,
Coins quickly release our pockets
From the weight and traffic of noon
We all return to, as words we collect
And store in the giant mailbox of the day.
Rain comes and slides the sweat
Off my forehead, a trickle of silence
Slips through the patter of entanglements.

Moving across a continent of yellow green
Land and waste, the river runs through
The country a spontaneous current of sound.
There is a bridge that crosses
The threshold of evening.
Each day l settle your face into the blanket,
The stars shine for me the miracle of your breath,
I see an opening in the hole
For us to swim through. We wear the joy
That floods our heart in the face.
There is no replacement for the warm
Eye that embraces the world.

CERTAIN AVENUES

New York City's harbor supports a slate gray sky
A steady drizzle impounds the landscape

Bricks fall on your head, and they are bricks

It's difficult to hide from the madness
To sit down with peace for a moment

These gray waters are your home
The prints on the wall, the hands of the clock

How do you escape from smokestacks
That smudge the canvas sky

The particulars of an April evening
Cast in the liquid light

Sifting the fine grains on your tongue
To open other avenues, to release the poorest material

ALONG THE RAILS

Armed with books,
I walk through
the shallow landscape
each fire creates.
The exact measure
of time weighs heavily.
The sun has broken out
of its three day gloom,
just in time
to write this poem.
It's 3 o'clock
of a February afternoon,
and I am burning
in this heavenly bush.
The gray city brushwork
spreads against the sky
like the tousled hair
of a madman.
I am that madman,
and this is our city,
stretching for miles
on an invisible wire.
What is the thread
that connects us
to a thin hope
along the rails to the future?
My footsteps retreat
into memory, like a swimmer
going backwards.

Susan M. Schultz

THE LOST COUNTRY

After the long siege, you lose
Empathy for the unguarded many, of whom
You were recently one, inebriate with danger
So constant it seemed artificial.

I think a lot about the line between
Suffering with and suffering for;
The preposition demarcates
Impossibility, a kind of suffering
I refuse to feel. Do I mean by feeling
Something self-conscious, something
Chosen as no one chooses this city,
Its walls breathing spite like history,
Making me into one I barely recognize?
The self's a tyrant, as is necessary
To maintain your poise where loss is
So profound you fail to see it
In the mounds of rubble just cleared
From the lot next door. The colony
By the sea proves that beauty's
Just a screen for horror; naked men
Shiver from the cold wind off the water,
And our phrases are too often repeated to mean
Even the platitudes of sympathy we intend.

Quite possibly, memory *is* the first art,
But only if aesthetics grafts itself to pain,
The jays' sharp chatter met by higher
Registers and the dull bleeding sound
Of the truck in the next road: all
The cacophony that resembles our failure
To speak. Perhaps it's best to invite failure
For a while, reserve the right to silence

Until words return, bubbling upward
Like lava, spelling a vocabulary of terror
And redemption before the next dispensation.
To be one within the stream
May mean the rush of syllables
Can give us life, if we give in
To another's empathy for us: language
Only saves itself, but full immersion in it
May save us from ourselves.

II.

Apprehension is the most agile mode of feeling,
Gaining ground like a new river writing itself
Forward, ever forward, not knowing where it's going
But always worried about it. What is there to fear
But one's own form? And who's to care
Unless it's you, paralyzed by the passage,
Afraid to read further except in digressions,
Happier prose than most, knowing themselves
Unworthy of our attention, but beaming between
The spotlights, stealing the show. How will
I remember this, the clutch of trees behind
The house, the frantic sound of leaves dis-
Placed by grackles, jays in search
Of mites, and all the lost hum of what
And how I thought about these things?

What stories there will be to tell — only
Time will tell, and I'm not there yet;
The present calls us home and there's little
We can do to change the order of our words
Despite the dam on the river that makes light
Of the water gathering behind it,
A mirror so like a map I'll never tell
The difference. Is thinking of this
Romantic, though partially crazed,
The reflex scare of the scene as you forget it?
The self a spinning top, gaining speed

Even as it loses momentum, and this
A definition of tragedy that's only slightly
Against the grain, where one's reflection
Can no longer show, as it shrinks into
The mere self of itself. Everything finally
Gets sealed in like a lion inside a hoop,
Stalled there because the mind chooses it,
Lost finally at the very apex of its leap.

III.

The wind reminds us of ourselves;
The trees in this equation are nouns,
The wind verbs, transitive at that,
And transitory, shedding the husks of leaves,
Bits of paper, fallen nests, though not
Revealing its core; only the rind
Of the wind shows. We may be past
Such equations of ourselves with things,
But our correspondence tells us otherwise,
That the words we shed like leaves
Do not conform to the shapes of sentences.
The house we share is a vocabulary,
And our struggles to stay in the same dialect
Are made more difficult by the way
In which words break, like shingles;
Repeated use merely reaffirms the difference
Between what we say and how the books
Tell us to say it. Words have dominion over us
As the tops of trees do over shadows
That play on the glazy surface of our yard.
The language recycles itself but is never the same
Twice; even clichés change
And that we trust them only means
We distrust stability, as we do
Any history that happens before our birth.
Try to re-capture what was never
In the first place captured; barring
That, create from point zero something

You always suspected was true,
Like the wind inside a jar, always abstract
And never there.

IV.

Distance is the face of the wind
Turned back to see what it just left,
And proximity has no face, unless it's yours,
Which I see as obverse metaphor
For what is literally true,
The slope of sunlight a dustmote climbs
As if it were the ladder to a firmer sight,
Unaligned with sadness or aught else
There is that can't be seen, but felt.
That's why the act of defining things
Is so necessary, even as it passes
Into obscurity, the slipped disc
Of the sun declining into a marsh
Whose water is as flat as paper,
Though not so sheer. What we feel
About this is not clear, words clotting
As soon as formed, but making a field
In which to talk about it; nothing
Else holds us together and yet nothing
Is so difficult to remember as pain,
Which is like a lake whose shores
Denote the difference between pain
And what it teaches us, the art
Of recollection without reliving,
Wisdom as the applied memory
That mediates between the present
And what constructed it, the past's most
Certain contingencies. Have we got
To the point where poems think
Out their implications, not stopping
For sunsets or even the dislocations
Of place, which refigure the self
In ways we can never know? Or is
There no thinking but in music,

The force of counterpoint like an ever-
Moving system, never stopping, even
For history, which is the substance
Of time without its spirit?
Sometimes I balk at the thought that
Poems create anything apart from themselves
Except the momentary glimmers
Of feeling so undefinable they may not
Exist outside intuition, the sideways
Surfaces of words turned like rear-view
Mirrors to catch the sight of nothing
But what the wind does, scattering
Leaves and sunlight on the concrete
Like shadow-boxers. The shifting currents
Of sadness and happiness are less
Shared than shareable, the yellow plain
Of being together where nothing finally settles
But sunlight, like the flakes of food
In a fishbowl, sifting downward
From surface into depth,
A metaphor so simple it must be true.

V.

Late morning — none of the animals in the yard
Is content; from all corners there come
Screeches, and the dull monotone
Of a territorial imperative
Somewhere being violated . . . by me?
I feel immune from the danger
That narrows to a symphony of noise
As overhead helicopter and airplane
Contribute their piece, until silence seems
The barest nostalgia. Abstraction
Is the mind's own silence, retreat
From danger, the predator's cave,
And when I go there I hardly notice
What it is I'm leaving: the thought
Of leaving you for now, an old fear

That what one leaves one loses
— How much easier to write that pronoun
As if by fiat one could transcend
The selfishness that still defines us,
Self-creation having no rules
But those we write as we go along.

VI.

As these lines go on they lose
Their substance, as cities their suburbs,
Gathering strength for the inevitable
Implosions and inept expositions
That lack a landscape. No
Landscape finally is necessary,
Though it gives us names for who we are
And doesn't tease us with the promise
That we share the land with others; hence
The loneliness it offers,
Desolate even in the midst of plenty.
For what we take of the land
We can never give back
Except in the names we affix to signs
That mean less than we want
Them to mean. Always someone
Was there before us, taking away
What had never promised to be
Ours, like the Ohio rivers
That wend their way through valleys
Dotted by the shells of houses,
Trailers, the paraphernalia
Of rootedness without its reasons.
Someday the land will forget,
Thrusting us into the limelight
And casting us out like first
Travellers, into the hidden valleys
Where we will be content,
Though free of words, which swim
Through the humid air like hawks.

VII.

Ovid must have felt the irony
Of exile for one who no longer wanted it,
Virtue in the language of the markets
Reduced to its negative in the clear air
Of the islands, white houses set like teeth
In a jaw that knows silence not as the lack
Of speech but as its substitute, the way
The exhilaration of roller-coaster rides
Comes to replace the near-ecstasy
Of the heretic who can't abandon
The old language of the church: Latin
Dusted our shoulders like butterflies,
Threatening decadence with origins,
Substituting our history for ourselves.
Having learned to praise, we forget
The inevitable mediocrity of origins:
Instances of doubt we refuse to name,
Choosing to hold to the old stories
Of conquest, deserts crossed and then
Forgotten, like those who show us
Not heroes born of conflict
But emblematic standers-in,
Being in division for its own sake,
Because we cannot do otherwise, knowing that
The sun never sets twice in the same
Way, except when you give memory
Access to the desire that exacts
A toll for every image it delivers.

VIII.

Spontaneity and sorrow: I used to think
Them linked as by an umbilical that draws
The continuous present into disjointed
Futures, where what's past is best
Remembered with regret, the perverse nostalgia
In which one loves the past precisely
Because it could have been better lived.

An odd disjunction arises between my old
Self — so long at the center of things,
Careering off-course as effectively
As a race car with a broken axle —
And my present one (certainly not new,
Just more consistent) who's losing
Contact, nay faith, with and in its past
Incarnations. Thank goodness, you might say,
There's so much archeology to perform
As from a clear platform that abuts the sea,
Acknowledging distance only
As an ancient rite, yet enjoying
It no less. Perhaps such pedantic visions
Are merely prologue to the epic
That comes after, when the desired
Exile is restored, literal this time,
Not some further ism of the mind.

IX.
Whatever we remember of farmland
We forget it here, where grapevines tease their wire
And miniature apple trees, likewise tethered,
Give off the scent of flowers that promise
But do not yet deliver; roses, the merely
Decorative, climb up the wooden gazebo,
Installed like a sentry box above
The lower fields. Nearby a spring burrows
Through the hill, a clear vein, and it takes
Work to see how simplicity becomes
So strange, so in cahoots with all
The subtle grammar of the seasons
And how we ever forgot this, immured
To a landscape rendered more strange
By our presence, making words
To govern it, as the frame of a picture
Implies closure, even if you know
There are other fields to walk, and love
The complexity of simple things. Take this

Bumblebee, its traffic pattern evident, though
Unmeasurable, stitching an invisible cord
Between the pollen's collocations. Or
The young brown bird with white breast
That follows its parent, screaming for food
As if there were no other anywhere
Who needed more than this reward.

Abstraction, then, is either too easy
Or too difficult; must be implicated
In the radical fact of the world,
Its gardens no emblem of simplicity
But an achieved grace, camouflaged
By our willingness to accept it
At face-value, and to read ourselves
As the players on its stage; no wonder
It takes so long to know oneself at all,
Since we are less categorical than inspired
By the categories themselves; no throw
Of the dice is unexpected, and nothing
Anymore astonishes, although
We've long ago been estranged
From every assumption there ever was.

MOTHERS AND DINOSAURS, INC.

In any case, if a strike's
called, you'll have to leave
home, all but your platitudes,
that is, base camps of comraderie,
the macho at the heart of passed time —
if it's considered national,
or natural: bagpipes
remind me we're all ethnics,
at least those men who wear
skirts are, not to skirt
the subject, but puns do tell
us something, who's on first,

that is, or who flicks the switch,
beats the clock to bed. What
ifs are history's best stories,
which even those in pin-stripes
knew as they logged in runs and
dodged questions. Panels convene
on such matters, weigh evidence
and tip their salary caps;
to the victors go the stats.
Quilting bees are left uncounted,
organized patchworks of cloth
and words, wise yarns that bind
an avenue of strangers. Not national
these binders of the unsewn,
unseen reapers of rags (ladders
where they start not found
in romantic scrapbooks filled
with might-have-beens or maudlin
trades at Peter's gate, where
I'm told this story ends).

I'll confess a need for origins,
even those bought from catalogues,
though knowing my grandmother's
skin was soft produces affect
only in inverse proportion to
her presence, dignity's distance
on a midwest veranda, before
I knew the words for place
or providence. That's ideology,
no doubt, the self's precarious
cartographer; now I see beauty's
often no more than fragility
realized. Know sentiment
strongest when least held to,
like books sold at auction
whose very pages smelled
Shakespearean. Time, like its
objects, is vain — glorious

too the way it spells
its name, the crook of early
English f's, frail teamwork
of double-ss's built into
systems as the lack thereof.
Now that's democracy, saith
the prig, aware of a process
made possible only in computer
versions of actual diamonds
in the rough. Who gets cut is
a team's prerogative, but
who remains is pure accident,
fired synapses returning
to their farm team as memory's
final loss. The borders open,
doubt's traffic synoptic, and
adoration's tagged as mutual
recognition. At strike's end
soliloquies will bloom again,
as to dust we return, rounding second.

THE PHILOSOPHER'S CHILD

In the year of the snake, rivers
flowed circuitously to sea; desire
for revenge filled the populace
with an inverse longing for balance
at any cost, like a field of grasses
that appeared only when the death
camps closed. Rabbits fled
the deadly suburbs, leaving only
a slight afterglow of gentleness;
theirs was an intermingled music
of chaos and counterpoint.
A dog walked these last streets,
and his memory brought him back
to a gutted house, stranded
in the white heat of a late sun.

Tigers roamed the city; through
the jawless face of the Central
Bank, I saw an ox run away, past
the monkey's mad graffiti, his paintings
of a lake country where trees leaned
waterward with maternal intent;
a boar fell in love with this country
and longed to take his family there.
The rooster was not inclined
to accept this outcome, wanting
to riffle his feathers against
a backdrop of rubble and waste,
unaccustomed to color and the rainbow
destiny of rain; so he sealed a pact
with the horse, whose legs carried
her through this antique city;
its gates were the wrecks of gas
stations, pumps standing like sentinels
over broken windows and abandoned cars.
Only the rat felt at home; his larder
was stocked with old butter, bread crusts,
curdled milk, and old asparagus heads;
the screams of children rang in his ears
like songs, earth warm with the residue
of fires, and that absentee landlord,
Sun, turned his dull eye elsewhere.

Here one couldn't distinguish origin
from end, history from the sublime
moment of its disappearance, slow
armageddon of artificial suns
and the sweet breath of dragons.
These sent their radiance back
to an imagined source, and their mouths
bloomed open like peonies. Horoscopes
told of a year of turmoil and strange
happiness, as of days past grief, the new
world opening to a redemptive clangor
of carnivals, now lodged at the city's edge,

where barkers and clowns called out. One
small child gave answer, waving from the burnished
frame of a burned out window, her tears
a kind of reverence expressed as interrogative.

DRIVE *ME*
for John and Rebecca Ernest

Maine fog, grizzled as the elder's
beard, fragile as an Oppen line, is
sufficient to forestall. That
is what I miss, both levity
and the duskness meandering meaning
becomes (I would not dispense with,
if I could not for that moment
hold it as pure as after–shower's
glow, drop unsettled, flower petal
bent, Benedict among the legions),
whose spirit blurs light to cloud,
vanquishes what there is that is
definite, definable in this parish,
the thought of which is bounty.
If faith sustains, then what is it
maintains belief? — bull in a crowd
of fighters, surmounting swords
until reflex tires. That after-
thought is text that comes before
a last crisis, and so resembles
forethought, though it procrastinate.
Bonfires consume a fjord's dark mirror
through which I saw not, but heard
waves murmur — Back out of my fog,
the sea's gray chin jutted: I told
you my toe nearly dropped off in
Lake Superior, though that's not
where the name comes in; it would have
been the same in Erie or Michigan,
errant thought indeed. Fact

purchases wisdom as tact produces
virtue like the piano's middle
pedal, its glottal stop; only
sound is sostenuto, even when
it's underfoot. Then let thought
BE music, mind's semaphor unspelled
but pointed out, meaning something
between word and sentence, instance
and repetition. No instant truth but
recognition, postcard junks alive
in Hong Kong harbor just as green
fishing boats skim the clotted fog,
New England's hard accent imitating
brevity, or bringing it about. Its
harbors are at once industrial
and "picturesque," and a tourist's
eye retains more than it ought,
scanning a city's syntax ably
as the bridge that now draws up
allowing commerce to commence.

PAGES FROM AN IMAGINARY ESCAPE

Festooned abstraction
    the bridge mirrors the mind.

To leap from there to sky

flooded with sun beams,
girders, air space

"permanently" gulping "instantly",
"instantly" gulping "instantly"

Then what of the bridge?

Brigge, brugge, log, beam, stick
hence wooden causeway
to provide a way across

Tightly strung web tensed in the haze

between elevated observer
and pedestrian palisade

The strings of an instrument tingling to be touched

Each flare of perception
a lonely peregrination
of the formless into form

A fulgurating synthesis
arched over a rush of broken bones

———

Pour of traffic,
        a river over a river under a stream.

Beam: to give out shafts of light
and *baum,* a tree.

Pore: originally a passage, a channel.

As in the unbearable moment in which the eye
seeks out something excluded from the scene

Then dislodged from its socket
is flung into the froth

The goddess known as "active tongue",
        as "ravenous mouth"

Smoothly takes
all things ripe and heavy
in her hands,

Barely perspiring
guides them
to her namesake.

Still enveloped,
        like fruit sucked by its own skin,
these self-same things
        tremble before the altar.

O sun whore
destroy this field
of pores —

hold my health in your mouth
and I will pay for it in words

finger the imagination's furnace
        palus a stake
or the fate of the palisade at stake

demand I flood you
          holy harlot
and I'll forget my name

at the top of the tower
where water wets the seeds

a language made to
rise from the language
like sap

engorged glades of river life
wave their sticky heads
as if on spindles

blue sky, white clouds
the sun aglow
with the semen
it has sucked

fellatio to
festival
to *perpetual feast*

makes up a world where there is none

———

Mist wound tight
around the portal

each phoneme
at play for me

to imagine anew
a reference

its assigned/unassigned
think now of a tugboat plowing upriver

and a theory of imagination
that predates both the perception

and the river

a theory is a fruit
a fear and a binding

a boat moving up a river
at biblical speed

An auditory replaces an ocular vocabulary
and the mind leaves off its mirroring.

As for the need of a transition:

Beneath the muffled engines of the commuter caravan
beneath the black chirps of the cicadas

if you listen with greater care

An armada of other worlds sails
into your quarantine in the here and now

At the edge of indeterminacy
someone has recently revived galleons

Firing cannons at the here and now

Prideful vessels that transport
sunlight from one lifetime into the next.

Or else two shores
at either end of an evidential gap

Rain falling
on the apparition of a bridge

From the topmost leaves
the drops run off

As an invisible foghorn sounds —
when this run off and that foghorn are one

Comes an instant of "gradually"
soothing the senses —

Airy abstraction that bursts
into moisture and tone —

Is not lost in the ancient world
     time as a structure of beauty.

———

The remedy for my bouts with suffocation:
the wind as it rattles the air
at altitudes above the encampment

Blue mirror, perforated veil

heart as sudden as a train-whistle

in a prior space of contemplation
where, to exaggerate, objects are so rarefied
they are not there if you aren't.

How odd, that when the architecture is dwarfed
     the mind goes free

But that this can only happen
from the tops of other edifices

Building giving distance to building
in a supersession of views.

To insist *in all this labor,*
          only ourselves
deprives the making of its mystery

and yet I admit

the tale *is* entirely human in its sailing,
a vessel of light anchorless and aglow
          in the already engineered

A porthole looking out
over our own estrangement

A map of projections in a book
beside other printed matter.

But such is also an ideal
of rising joy, the transport
of a figurative sustenance

Next to which the natural and the divine
are seen as a telling out of one

Auto-intoxication, auto-immolation,
  automobiles, bumper to bumper
on the bridgeway below

"A felt architectonics then
          of the numinous"

Pictures and unpictured thought

Loft of vision, telepathy of wires

     Patience its antithesis, the infirmity of conviction.

———

Achilles bestride the cliffs

forgotten his human side

ear turned from the sea —

divine without knowledge of the source

Thetis as hidden as a pearl

to the rage of his projections.

Violence regales the sky,

the sea, both shores;

sharks teeth glimmer

on the river's waves.

To kill — what?

The world sacrifices itself

to its own image.

———

The Washington Bridge, completed October 25th, 1931:
The great cable towers of the bridge rise 335 feet into the air, two and a third times
as high as those of the Brooklyn Bridqe, Thus in 50 years the physical scale of
engineering has more than doubled itself, as may be seen also in the relative length
of the main river spans of the two bridges, 3500 and 1600 feet.

A nightly drilling into rock and lichen:

through labor
the instant is worked
into the repository
of "was", "is", and "will be"

in leisure this grid holds

beyond labor and leisure
    no time to speak of.

Capitalism and its accretions:

a dream of knowledge
that presumes a verifiable future

an act of perception
that takes as its tactics the here and now

the suck of experience
that draws us towards a preestablished past

beyond these
no one dares speak —

the promised eternal doubling —

lest articles of faith founder on the edge of lore.

———

A transcript of what happened Somewhere Else

Above all, that is the time that must be spoken with

Against the wishes of the demiurge

That creative being who sings like the Sirens

An apt metaphor for God.

North American rapture on the dole

By dint of advertisement's kill of language,

Awaken from your shipwreck!

Bright light and drowned-out canoe,

Global gods and goddesses that used to clash

Believing falsely they could not die,

Tomorrow's sky chopped into quadrants:

All forms are fragile when countered by force

Force a form too but not the first.

Pore: originally a passage, a channel, a tiny mouth

Limbs refracted into ribs and cables.

Not the energy behind all commerce and consumption

Not the right to shop at Shop Rite

Or to rend one another limb from limb

But the American knowledge that all that arises

Arose so recently

There once was another time

A spiritual principle to be applied to the present

Without romanticism —

To wit,

To go forward hesitantly into the betterment.

———

"The orchestration of sun and sight
has been other on every morning
since reaching the newly discovered land" —

words attributed to an early explorer
            previously undiscussed

let us call him Vasco Pajama.

"The seagulls are larger and more white
than the seagulls at home,
the waterways more wet.
I think we have reached some great pleroma."

"Perhaps if we continue inland some more years
      all we've left behind will seem imaginary
and these surroundings our norms"
      continues Pajama
in a late log entry
just before bedding down.

But the next morning he returns
to the earlier trope:

"the unknowns always outweigh the knowns"
      and
"So what if in my sleep I no longer see the womb?
New territory is also an interior unfolding."

In fainter script:

"For my log alone:
I have worn the mask of greed
   only to please Queen and crew,
   have no desire to rule over all
   — or any — of what I view.
May no one ever follow my lead into these parts
for with the crowd come thirsts for goods and God,
      the failure of my perfect escape.

Let everything here remain strange and I the stranger.
To be disoriented is to be filled with love."

Soon after this the Pajama party
disappeared into the sleepless void.

Pajama had discovered America.

———

Clytaemnestra bestride the metropolis

that in all its formal rectitude and size

resembles Agamemnon writhing in his net —

accursed house of mastery, enslavement, and slaughter

the coast of this or any other North American town.

Revenge does not so much befoul as bequeath

its progeniture a cause and effect no one kept in mind.

Orestes unborn (not seen), Orestes in exile (not seen),

Orestes standing over his murdered mother

a mouth to suck his hands of self-renewing blood.

Yes, here are the snapshots in the family

tabloid, the ones you've developed. And Justice ?

— Athena, jury, they do not convince

or relieve the mind of the hot flash of injustice

just as an end does not conclude

but only makes a new beginning —

Not in absolution or punishment carried out *pro forma*

can the accursed cycle leave off from murder

but only by the construction of a negative time and place

unforeseen archipelagos in the hindmost stars

a considered staging   a veiled intoxication

beyond the pages of an aborted escape

   and the slaveship's stinking holds

Eleni Sikelianos

THUS, SPEAK THE CHROMOGRAPH

The night we discovered
that a thing could be more

than True, and more again
than False, a thing could carry its name

with a ticket of lights called
Possible: We were

in contempt of the Law of All
Excluded Thirds, and the sky

for example, continued to pile up
clouds without account, a mass of gasses with numbers

under them. I knew this to be
written in the Book of Weeds, a treatise on leaving

the house at dusk, when all buildings have already had time enough
to fit themselves back into shadows. As if there were only:

dusk-to-dusk, between dusk-and-dust
where no animals asserted themselves

as separate from the day, and the night
comes again, as it always

had done. We could not follow
the map — because the Book

of Nature was written
in math's un-
certain language, author of black

rains, why the naked
eye
unclothed
can see

between math's limits
why

a baby's bones are soft
as pudding when first let out
of the water & take

a long time
to harden, you can flatten
a newborn

's skull by placing it
on a board, the death-hole
of the cranium takes

6 months to close

and then grow brittle

(How long it took to understand rivers
run toward the sea)

J(OY)'S THE AIM (essay)

It sounds like a war outside the Tuileries.
They are digging up the garden & we can hear it from the hole.
The day will wrinkle

into the dream where A. was leading us through trees. (There) we were
                                                    lost of us, boxed
between the poplars, with no room in between. When was I

torn to the clear
a spirit absent to itself
from tenebrous force

nocturnal thickness of a brilliant childhood packed into nights
and days endlessly repeating — who never made
a pact with shadows or light

Evenings, dusk fell on like a blanket of sad riding me
or my bike through the fog

to erase all trace of before or after
(in a simultaneity of words) to darkly confirm the fissures
in such a solid existence

It was just the atoms and flesh that held up for the moment or to it

It took one unit of logic to discover
the non-existence of god or the world & a million
to flush it out. I was involved

in forensic relations
with angels, there were ghosts
on Canon Perdido near the handcrank washtub and under
the ubiquitous apple tree

Dreams of a ruined state had not yet taken body

Who put the plug into humans
I could find none
common measure nor
take body
to chase night into day

I will take all responsibility for my birth
I was my own accomplice & adversary
I must sting the light as

it soon appears that being born
is an infinite proposition, a crisis I

suffered in verbs
in the limits where a word can enter
into relationship with another word
(things with things), a heart

heated to white-hot, a virgin eye thrown over
the scientific perfection of the world, prey to the 'green
membranes of space' or a 'crystalline ray
from the center of earth' which hits mid-body

I was brung to the human ladder
& dreams fell asleep
on all my bodies . . . Then, & I was young: Suddenly.

IN A PRE-RAPHAELITE LIGHT

Let me remain still
in the ice-fair, the true blank
of an eye

athwart the heart
as a puny tilter

E. — is
nothing am

Copse me in these

fits, Rose,
at an instant. Lame me with it.

Make a testament
as worldlings go—to rush an atom; I'm so full of matter— rushing the barrier

of psychological speculation— Rush,
abandoned of the velvet friends

Heave off
These small animals cluttering earth

Hem away, boys,
to kill them up

& tie this leaden note
unto the sweet bird's throat

THE DECAMERON

Don't think in sleep I am
absent

in this repeating

NIGHTS

as in

NAMES

owe nothing

to me; Don't think

I am ready

to be skeletal AGE

glued to my neck BUT

WHAT am I here blind to (for)
I am always blind

to something i.e. Everything
we see is made up

of 90 chemical
elements tunneling

thru the energy barrier

and a blue square applied to the body of the EARTH:
and if they said; here; live here; six billion of you; and
we did; ready

to smile in the morning and shed tears at night; and tomorrow and in
                                                    the evening and
the next day again;

(caesura)

To the fireball that started off
the universe some
15 billion years ago: Hello

to us with origins in dust

THE BRAMBLES OF CAVALRY (QUAMASH)

        the ana-
        cardiacious sumac
            mango

        pistachio and
                varnish trees
        is missing

a center between
        the diverging
branch

of the river which loses itself
        in sand and

and the events
which were misplaced

in time, the fruit

of the family being likened
to a bird's heart might
        be one way to speak

about proton explosions 60

tons under
the waters of

        TNT . . . I.e.:

A, H, an alphabet of bombs
invented beneath deserts & unfolded

in limbs in the wings
of cities. A to Z, a compendium

of the wearers of theorems in scarlet

numbers. They have hermetically sealed
the mouths of the bearers of wonders & the trash

cans in this city, each a badge of
light, a rubbish-

incited lock-down. In the cave of St. Desire
I was saved from the clutch

of matter Before
we learned to eat

the death camass
in the deep woods off I repeat

this train
will not leave

the station, the night-
tortoise riding an iron

horse, & spit-
shining the floor. In the dream
we were trying to make a word-

garment between alpha
and o. for before we wore

the warbelt inside out
but the Letters

the letters would not fit.

POEM

My eye can't fix you

in the whole white

nuance of light

or

Astonish myself to find you

such as I am; swimming

in humanity; separated from each

by a field delimiter; who rises

to look for the light-socks folded

into a satin stain-drawer;

I warn you: Nothing solid

is built on me; I can't design

prudence for the first time

Each day, from my joints

I raise toward you

the accents of a humble pain

Stop this commerce

Stars belong to you

Because you know the detours
of a heart; (Shut up or) Tell me

from *UNBRIDLED*

:

watch

each articulation, each

relation in the golden rotation

of the Achilles tendon – spin

with the 14 rotations of the crystal spheres

REMINDING THE TREES the world exists in seven

even spaces I find myself in Seven

deadly eyes,   children speaking

in hospitals,   mouths opening

wide,   the inside

            needles

                        plunging

            sweet

    dying men in pale skin

        greying to that other world, bright ash

amongst the tears

of old men waiting:

we are what we were

        still moving through what we know from what

        we've been told

          bones without a body

          light without a source

          housing for electric:

The old women talk in the back

room. (Now let them dream awhile.)

       * * * * * * * * * *

'AGE HAS ITS TEETH FALL OUT'

with 'MORE GOLD THAN HE IS WORTH' & what

of the radiant world

that turns its rays to a thousand roads — ?

          sailing in violence (to meet it)

          press the eyes

          (despite the palm of red)

           be polite to the woman at the counter

When light gets trapped

into becoming matter

the dog-broke day follows the day

(Here) (I am again) smiling at passengers

(Here) (We are again) (smashing) (or) (anchoring) lights. 'Tonight

nobody

is going anywhere.'

Rod Smith

from *IN MEMORY OF MY THEORIES*

XCII (cinder-sifter)
for Peter Gizzi & Liz Willis

Heigho, says Anthony Rowley
                  hedgehog
But a hedgehog in a pin-cushion
        the one, I hear, to nurse
        in ten you have three
A Hill full – a hole full
All begins with A
        fill the hall, nobody
"Indeed I have not any
        in its flower, and ignorance
About the bush, my moppet
I'll meet thee alive.
        As the fish
Is fair and wise and good and gay
        as simplicity scattered became
I'll go to Newcastle
        to be filled wish Oh!
        like a valley to melt
And a child is born on the Sabbath day
            "Hoogh," quoth he.
"Honey," quoth she
        (in an)
        . . . bamboo slips
& went his way in other men's ditches
        gradually a valley obscure
Put your finger in your eye
            holy inner latter
Sing holly, go whistle, and ivy
        The difficulty of
        treasures

                        heart the latter tastes
Sing ivy, sing ivy
In Fife and his wife
            nature is exactly abstruse
I do not know and I do not care
Seven as six close five who four.
                    I alone confused.
My father left me three acres of land
They walked on their feet
            the multitude, smart multitude
Sing ivy
            does not quieting smile
A hundred eyes, and never a nose
      in its movements chooses time
Noddle merry with merry merry with
                        head. in the bottom spiritual
And a child is born on Sabbath day
            bright bright I
In his hand each land — and feet
Is fair of face, and giving
                    To help them Heaven death
Here we go up, up, up,
Thumpaty, thumpaty, thumb!
            Extreme fondness surely wastes
Rain in under the dark
            crooked seems its summons
"Will you have any more?"
"My eyes are too sore."
Frumpaty, frumpaty, frump!
            there is none his mouth
Is telling his beads
            the common sin   Motion
Among the green weeds
                    he blunts
                            he shuts
Can I get there by candle-light? —
                    with non-diplomacy
To see the Parliament soldiers pass
            horses race curbs

Get you gone, with a round body, what's that?
                    war clumsy
                              contentment
Left in a wood, and there a prod
                    inclining tone
                    [one's] person only limits desire
But Ringman cannot dance alone
                    voice
Hide, horn and all
                    only the after
Shall have a little bit.
No lark as blithe as he.
                    — everlasting end —
                    of the body
And sow will l have mine
                    the eternal stupid
                              saved his mouth affairs
I took the marrow-bone, and beat about his head
                    historian
On New Year's Day in the morning.
And when they got home shared the booty together
                    gaudy colors to carry sharp words
"Then pounce, pounce," says every one
                    a gem to be let down
"She's down, she's down" says every one
          reason's motion   is reason's function
                    the low foundation
And the jackass's load
                    we honor the left
Cuckoo, cuckoo
                    in unpropitious affairs
But John Ball shot them all
the assistant the evasive the reverting
Their wings are cut
What I've got, you have not
                    it stands and changes
                              imaging its limits
& singing such a funny song
                    name but different

               because they live among soldiers
Tommy laughed, and found his face
Blowsey boys, bubble O
        The tiger of a growth
A hill full — a hole full
        is scanty easily scattered
All of a row
            while they exist
They think that I'm gone mad
        That mind is at rest
        contentment despised
Sing holly, go whistle, and ivy
        most tender surely
        itself to intend them
        the world's model, the eternal returns
For you never shut your eye
        glory does not injure doing
As the day lengthens,
So the cold strengthens.
Sing ivy, sing ivy
        [Who] knows

(*illegible*) LAKE
for Jonas Berry

The frames they extract tone
individual competence. Acre
as *opposite*. The lattice inhabits
an inexact outer circle. The ballistic aspect
of the untoward composition's
nonsense description. Its richness.
My lilies in the pan have revived
with the cooler weather since the
rain. Bulbous, gemlike, molecular,
mind, control. (It rained last night.)
We return having to them with this
promise, to textualize the offense,
the affiliation — This is what they require
that they may keep. Tired slop of law
& nowadays arms & legs only at long long
intervals an irksome coherent bafflement.
They act first to the shore, though
the waves, Deep Cut, do not run much,
nor coincide — a fundamental jurisdiction
in the icon's difficult resolve — *it* rather
cordially, and so forth. The degree of mistrust
magnifies the measure of abstraction.
The lightning is an exaggeration of the light.

ABSOLUTE VARIABLE SWITCHING STRUCTURE

granaries

        The old

      Earth follows

    to be put to.
       resemble

       listening

to

      keeps

    it not.

       feminise
            Unity duality trinity/nothing
moderation confusion/alas limits ceases/yet one's deaths/
companions die/rigid dry [auxiliary particle] strong strong
doomed/weaker enemy light/ Practice the not does not the distant

to the distance

      rows

    dull

    the little ocean
   confused in its addition

UNTITLED (STRANGE LOOP)

It has been good to think about Harry Truman this Spring and
Summer, After all, many a spoken You really means an it to which one
merely says you from habit, thoughtlessly, This is called the
photoelectric effect, Breaking through crust of habit to actual
perception, seeing something continually for the first time, The river
bay scenery, all about New York island, any time of a fine day — the
changing panorama of steamers, all sizes, often a string of big ones
outward bound to distant ports, By turning in and taking interest in
these feelings, he encourages the child to trust that he share all of
himself without worrying about being judged, criticized, evaluated, or
put down, a trust that is necessary to him to develop inner mastery
and the potential for intimacy, He does not even speak of himself, he
merely speaks "on his own behalf," It took the form of several hundred
random pulses, each lasting about a millionth of a second, and it was
all gone in about another thousandth of a second, . . . Now to eat if
one other can — and if we cant the girseau Q.C., Washpots prizebloom
capacities — turning out — re- placed by by the headpatterns my own
capacities — I was not very kind to them, It did not matter that there
was no national issue or popular grievance; the politicians would see to
that, and principles could be attended to after victory, Perhaps he
wrote of love out of fear of seeking it in life, That's what some of these
fellas that sit on the sidelines never seem to realize, that you have to do
your best to keep things moving, Much has happened since the
eighteenth century to shake this view and to show that, if it is to
survive at all, it must be modified, But it is hard to imagine how this
question, phrased in just such a way, can avoid having an eternal,
once-and-for-all aspect to it, But Sumatra had not yet been taken over
by the Dutch, and another local sultan, at Mukkee, had to be given the
same treatment before American ships could trade safely with
Indonesia, Yet because so much of what is distinctly human is so often
labeled "weak," and therefore rejected or denied or feared, it is
difficult for persons to own, value, or be in harmony with their full
humaness, And that is one of the reasons that when I got into a
position of power I always tried to keep in mind that just because I
saw something in a certain way didn't mean that others didn't see it in
a different manner, The way she says I — what he means when he

says I — decides where a person belongs and where a person goes, I
think that knowing to look at all and knowing what to look for is
rather a lot, Canada, however, could depend on Tecumsah's braves,
and the war was far from popular in the United States, The fact that
the poet does not meet the criteria of the above list does not really
seem very important, So I went out there, and I put a wreath on that
monument, and it seemed to work out all right, And thought, ever
obliging and skillful, paints with its accustomed speed a series — nay,
two series of pictures on the right and left wall, This raises difficulties
in biological studies, for high speed electrons tend to damage a
specimen, but then difficulties can be partly overcome by technical
tricks, and magnifications of over a million times have been achieved,
That made him a hero to the Whigs, but failed to change his views or
even make him a Whig, Not grasping fully the true nature of a concept
and its relationship to human experience, a person may still ask, "But
what about the poet, for example, is he not less masculine than the
athlete," I said that if that happened it would be a pity, but I had no
intention of running on a watered-down platform that said one thing
and meant another, And many a spoken It really means You whose
presence one may remember with one's whole being, although one is
far away, The Theory of Symmetries (mathematicians call it the theory
of groups) is highly developed, and since the doctoral thesis of Elie
Cartan in 1894, we have been aware of all the kinds of symmetry
possible, In the inside there is sleeping, in the outside there is
reddening, in the morning there is meaning, in the evening there is
feeling, There are even considerably different preferred distances for
standing during coversation among cultures, But looking back on
them, the years don't seem simple at all, It is the whole human being,
closed in its wholeness, at rest in its wholeness, that is active here,
These remarks are possibly more remote from any conceivable area of
everyday concern than any other statements in this book, and they
therefore have been placed at the beginning, The emphasis is
persistently centric, so that once one sought a vocabulary for ideas,
now one seeks ideas for vocabularies, The President declared, "This
defeats every purpose of my coming here," and stalked out, visibly
irritated.

for Lyn Hejinian

Juliana Spahr

spiderwasp
or
literary criticism

(a beginning)

He or she wants to write something called "Literary Criticism." It is about contemporary poems and poetics.

He or she begins.

He or she begins by telling the story of his or her difficult relationship.

(more powerful, smarter, quicker)

This is the plot of his or her narrative: things are outside the door.

Like the pepsis wasp that goes out at dusk and waits by the tarantula's burrow for the tarantula to come out.

The tarantula comes out to look, blindly, in the dark for a mate.

Things are outside his or her understanding. Like his or her passivity in the face of being buried alive.

Things are more powerful, smarter, quicker. Like a wasp that flies and understands his or her passivity.

There is nothing that he or she can do about this.

Things are there and he or she doesn't know what to do.

(the story unfolds)

The rest of the story can be summarized like this: a pepsis wasp must lay eggs on the body of a tarantula. The details are: he or she is beautiful and formidable; he or she is deep, shiny, blue all over. For each egg, he or she must provide one adult tarantula, alive but paralyzed.This is a story involving submission and dominance: wasp searches for correct version of tarantula (for only one version will do); as wasp searches it probes tarantula's body with an antenna; once right version is found, wasp digs grave for tarantula; tarantula stands by; wasp then returns to the tarantula, explores again, searching for the soft spot where the tarantula's legs join its body; there is a fight now and the wasp wins to paralyze the tarantula with poison, always wins; wasp drags tarantula to grave, attaches egg to its side, buries both, leaves.

(the story unfolds)

This is the story of metaphor.

This is the story of powerful masses — strong, healthy, capable of killing the minority of power — brought down by passivity, by desire only for leaving day after day, moment after moment behind, by ignoring, always ignoring the way the crafty wasp of capital controls reproduction.

This is the story of human relation — the one ripe with
reproductive desire outsmarting those out at night,
almost blind in the dark, looking for a mate.

This is the story of a foreign threat, the kind that flies
over the homeland, killing the naive, peace-loving, not
so poisonous, of us.

This is the story of how husband or wife or boyfriend
or girlfriend or most other relations interact

This the story of literary criticism.

(a comparison is made)

In the narrative, he or she is wasp and tarantula. Beau-
tiful and formidable. Deep and shiny and blue all
over.

What is meant by this is that he or she is more com-
plex than we can imagine. And this is how it is with
the arms, the legs, the body of one person and an-
other person. They are wasp and tarantula. They are
buried together and one is feeding off the other. They
are touching, touching, but not always in nice ways.
Or what this says is that they are always escaping their
confines. Or what this says is that the touch between
the arms, the legs, the body of one person and an-
other person is always narrative and subject to literary
criticism's analysis.

Here is what it is like when we read:

(arrives at the airport)

The literary criticism is the bridge is the moment
when he or she arrives at the airport to pick him or
her up.

He or she is not smiling when he or she arrives at the
airport to pick him or her up.

He or she is complaining about him or her not smil-
ing.

But he or she just wants to sit down and read the
newspapers that other passengers or people picking up
other passengers have left behind.

Everything has flipped to the other side. Like a book
held upside down.

He or she is flipped to just wanting to be there reading
the newspapers left behind by other passengers or
people picking up other passengers. Flipped from
wanting desperately to pick up him or her because he
or she missed him or her.

Everything has flipped to the other side.
Like a page.

Spider bites and flipped pages have happened. He or
she went away and came home and was the same he
or she only different.

He or she came home covered with spider bites.

(that evening, those next few days)

That evening, those next few days.

(a hinge, a page)

Like the wasp that searches for the tarantula, he or she searches his or her legs, arms, bodies.

He or she is trying to understand what the relation between him or her and him or her has changed into. A hinge. A page. A beautiful and formidable.

Are the choices production or reproduction?

Him or him or her or her?

(someone comes home)

He or she came home with his or her body covered with spider bites.

He or she came home with his or her shirt torn.

He or she came home.

The coming home is the opening of the book.

He or she came home and there was much crying.

There was much crying because he or she had had relation with another person.

Like in reading — its surprises, its perplexities.

He or she came home and he or she and he or she held each other all night.

He or she came home and the spider bites were the sign of being away, in a different climate, with a different body

He or she came home.

He or she opened the book and he or she confessed his or her anger.

He or she came home and read and confessed but also withheld much information and refused various rites of interpretation.

This upset him or her.

He or she came home and the arms, the legs, the body was different.

There was a breach in the relation.

The page was turned.

He or she came home and he or she and he or she were all confused.

He or she refused to tell certain things, making certain other things, the gaps in the narrative, more powerful.

He or she refused to tell certain things and thus made certain imaginative things all the more real.

He or she came home.

(a joined product)

So what he or she means to say here is that though reading is difficult, the spider bites, the crying, the breach, he or she comes home or two species combine but not in very pleasant ways and they contract and change and make room and this is the way it means to join and this is how things change between him or her and him or her and this how he or she remakes his or her arms, legs, body. As a new arms, legs, body. As a new product — one leg on the foot,

the other on the thigh, one arm around the back, the
other on the shoulders – a joined product. One thing
feeding off another thing. Buried. The story of this
joined product is the story he or she wants to tell in
"Literary Criticism."

But he or she is also worried that the comparison is
not working. There are so many factors – the taran-
tula, the hims or the hers, the wasps, the books, the
eyes, the words, the literary criticisms, the various
arms, legs, bodies. He or she is worried that too much
juggling is going on. But he or she is also convinced
that for literary criticism to have any hope of being
anything that does necessary work it must be capable
of juggling many different things. His or her relation-
ship with him or her and him or her and him or her.
Many lines of direction. The foot diagrams for a diffi-
cult and unusual dance that is represented on paper.
A child learning how to speak through stutterings and
gaspings. A threat paralyzed, an egg attached to its
abdomen. Him or her and him or her sitting on the
edge of the bed talking about how difficult it is for him
or her now that there are other hims or hers. A trian-
gle turning into a square turning into an octagon in
the kaleidoscope. Beautiful and formidable. Deep and
shiny and blue all over. Swooping. Sitting at the edge
of the bed.

(one thing?)

He or she wants to make this complexity of relation –
this complexity where one thing has dominion and
understanding over another thing all in one moment
but in another moment the another thing has domin-
ion and understanding over the thing – into a meta-
phor for how we encounter works and worlds. He or
she wants to explain the recent events in his or her life
as a comparison for what happens when one writes

literary criticism. He or she is often confused about how he or she feels about literary criticism. Whether he or she likes it, whether it has a use value, whether it is something good or not. But this makes the comparison continue to work. For the events in his or her life keep getting more and more elaborate, the connections with other people get more and more elaborate, and he or she is not sure how he or she feels about this elaborate.

He or she feels that encountering is abandonment, seduced and thrilled. It is that feeling of being beautiful and formidable, deep and shiny and blue all over. He or she feels that encountering is abandonment, probed and manipulated. He or she feels these things and sees this as what is important about them.

He or she continues to buy books and read them.

(everything has flipped)

In the comparison that he or she is using, the literary criticism stands for many moments when legs, arms, bodies touch. It is the hinge, the flip, the change in perspective. It is transition work.

Its pages are always opening, opening. It lines are always ending and returning. It is always broken open, broken open. It cries.

In relation one person takes a bit of another person, takes a fragment of that person, and lets it into that other person.

In literary criticism, the same thing happens.

Like a bridge that joins two things together.

(the literary criticism is the connection)

This is the story about a pepsis wasp who lays eggs on the body of a tarantula.

In writing about another person and his or her relation to him or her, in writing about a book and his or her relation to it, he or she writes certain words and these words refer to certain events. In the story of the tarantula and the wasp, the literary criticism is the connection this story has with his or her life, with how he or she is forced to wonder a lot about who is the tarantula and who is the wasp.

In the narrative he or she is looking for a body on which to plant an egg but only certain bodies make sense.

He or she and he or she tries to understand the sting which is much worse than that of a bee or a common wasp.

He or she tries to understand the bite which is not directed at humans and is dangerous only to insects and small mammals.

He or she reaches out and he or she explores him or her with his or her antenna, with his or her legs and belly

He or she shows an amazing tolerance.

He or she crawls under him or her, walks over him or her.

There is no hostile response.

The molestation is so great and so persistent that he or
she stands up, stands for several minutes.

So it is with the way he or she turns pages.

(we)

So it is with what is expected of all of us as encounter-
ers, readers, sleepers on the job, word counters, eleva-
tor operators, word processors, typists. With what is
necessary in the act of reading. With reading things
that are good and moving to us, good and moving to
our lives. We must attach ourselves to the abdomen
and feed. Joining has become a part of our lives. We
are growing into something and it is difficult. We are
missing the words or missing the boat or missing the
bridge by a few miles. It is like this. We are looking
for changing. We are joining things. We join our nar-
rative to other narratives, the narratives of prose or
poetry or articles in *Scientific America.* We join our
loves and others. We join relations. As a result we are
trying to write an article, a piece called literary criti-
cism about joining because in literary criticism we take
a piece of something, take fragments, and string them
together with our own commentary or commentary
that is in reaction to something else. The commentary
is designed to be narrative so as to cover up the frag-
mentary nature of quotation.This is the way it is with
thinking, with gendering, with joining. Forms can
carry all ethical positions, like people, all the positions,
all the meetings and dividings. We are transition work.

Chris Stroffolino

TO KEEP MEANING FROM
EMERGING FROM THE MESH

We meet like shoelaces
Knotted by a need that likes to act nonchalant
Staring its object straight in the threat I mean face . . .

Work and play, too, become
Another dualism abstracted from a unified sum
Like digging beneath the tulip
To find its roots in rain . . .

Work's like sunglasses
Somebody punched a lens out of:
We see both ways simultaneously.
The parallel lines my double vision saw
Have finally met in a blur . . .

Some days work's hell
But I'd have to deal with people anyway
The way desire dogs me around
And meaning's some scummy moralist, witty alien,
Poking his head out from the marriage bed
Charming us to keep our mind off his dissection.

Living, or dying?
Just 'cause we know the sand's
Being poured down the drain
Doesn't mean it doesn't *feel* immense,
And cannot, like running, be run away from.

So whether or not you get the job
Has much to do with romance
And whether or not you get to seduce
Depend's on whether a job's the excuse.

AS IF WE COULD EVER BE INTERESTED
IN WHAT'S BETWEEN THE POINTS OF INTEREST

I grasp at the straw that broke the camel's back
The short straw which is the needle in the haystack
Of the mind one tries to drive the camel through
For surely, the mind is a place you can only
Get to by car, but I'm a permanent (though not eternal)
Pedestrian going from the chair to the bed
As if I'm a jetsetter going from Nebraska
To Serbia-Croatia poof like that with a stop-over
In Djibouti where it's mandatory to feel like Sisyphus
In order not to feel like you're missing out on anything.

So the frankenberry amphetamine youth goes up
In the smoke from the cigarette you think I'm talking to
When I think I'm talking to you. As if the root
Precedes the seed. I cried when Kennedy died
But only because my diapers were dirtier than shit.
The 80's weren't the 50's so the 90's can't be
The 60's. But the 60's weren't the id after all,
Though this doesn't mean that I'm not dissatisfied
With the status quo, which I am (Mind you) but only
Insofar as the status quo is up in the air.
Of course, the hole in the ozone is up in the air . . .
If only Saddam Hussein or Neil Bush were the hole in the ozone,
Then I wouldn't feel guilty for not being lonely
The very night the Governor gives his cronies
Fat raises I can name and blame if that'd make
Anything that matters feel better.

I thought that what I thought was more like
What I felt than what I did was. But I thought
(or felt) that others would think that what I did
Was more like what I felt (and mattered more)
Than what I thought was. And dressing up like my
Superego when it thinks the only things that matter
Are in me, they yell. "Hey, pig, cripple, Mr. Substance-
But-No-Style, Mr. Signifyin' Monkee." having got my

Number by the balls, but I was too busy pretending
I was too busy to listen.
                              So is it easier for a left-hander
To become ambidextrous than a right-hander? Or did
John Lennon need McCartney as much as McCartney
Needed Lennon? Surely, I'm not running away
From the world, just running toward the self
(good boy you get an A). But the difference
Between personal and political only matters
if you side with nouns against verbs, if you
Can tell the difference between a corpse and a criminal,
Doctors and actors. If you're convinced that rapists
Preceded bras, women wouldn't have invented money
And toothpaste just happens to have sugar in it. . . .

Math becomes music when pain becomes spam.
The victory of drab over evil (yahoo).
if Hendrix would've lived longer, "Fire"
Would sound like "Raindrops keep fallin' on my head"
(which I don't totally hate by the way).
Funny how "As Nasty As They Wanna Be" is banned
In a state only obviously penis-shaped from the
Bird's-eye view we, most of us, ate for breakfast
Like our bones yeah try to shit them out. . . .

CIRCLE JERK

Circles are lies, tires leave tracks, the sun
Will die, there's a theory. If the enemy of
My enemy, say time, is not necessarily my ally,
Alibi or stooge, is that more thrilling or
True to the price paid for paradise than
The self merely erasing what erases it,
The water becoming the cup, and such?
Identifying not with what dies but with
What stays (and who says it has no eyes)?

Petrified, you can't walk out of the shadow
Of the skyscraper, but can only hope to see the sun
By being built taller. Trading effectiveness
For "realism" you, as usual, must tell off
The bird too excited to worry about coming
Home bloodied. "I want to be diverted" says
A detour. "Yeah, sure" replies the blindman
Who feels the straightness of the dipstick whose
Flexible limpness fooled the way I see it when placed
In the limpid water of the "world". There's a theory

About harvests being easier than planting,
About planting being easier than tending the
Field, about the virtues of sticking by
Your hometown team when it's not playing
As much as you do when it's getting paid
To lose, but the fact that I don't have to listen
To be silent doesn't disprove the fear
That all the solstice guarantees is the
U-turn of an abstract axis. There's a theory

The stillest rocks conceal the edgiest electrons,
The drummer is less conscious than the lead guitarist,
A guy feeding his cat less loving than a lion
Tamer. The map doesn't think as much as the
Cactus in the center useless as a convenience store
At noon. Ultimately as small as my worries, not
Defeated until dead (though every defeat is a death),
I love you til you're me, but that's fine
If I'm afraid around what I love. Oh, and how many
Times must the kid do what she wants before her
Parents stop saying "That's not you"?

As if the backstretch must be more authentic
Than the starting line that's the finishing line
Where all the fruit so sweet it's hard to digest
Is told there's no room at the inn where all
The curves life has thrown you are being ironed out
By the smoke of a momentary high impersonating

A once-and-for-all change which doesn't clear
Until the eye looks out to the hurricane (of the
Horizon it's beyond), the hurricane that would
Prevent it from writing about what I'm neither
Writing to, nor from: the circles you move in
That are out of my reach now.

TRADE OFF

if i want another chance
at seeing you for the first time,
i must murder memory's cozy
propensity for familiarizing
as numbers "tame" savannahs into streets.

if i want another chance
it's only because i assumed
memory allows thought without feeling
sets of eyes are all it takes
to start a fire sure as selves leak through;
the sluiceless noun i am in the sleep
that fears sleep never blinks.

who was the what that turned away,
put out the fire with some gasoline of
loss such leeches as the mind feeds on,
hearing the scream of your breasts
only on instant replay?

no way of preventing the past —
but if tomorrow digests yesterday,
the faultline on hold, can today
digest today? we might as well
chase our tails, eat our shit
& enjoy the feedback, getting off
on the warmth there's no we to feel
because that's too busy burning

a lie is watching it,
we can only assume it happens,
circle round it, as reflection
is preparation, the crow amid
the first snow of a midnight new year,
ostrich buried in the cocoon,
Stevens pacing his closet
while his wife, the liberty dime,
throws temper tantrums outside

getting it down is to make
sex into the self,
waves lapping at all sides
to idolatrize it,
"your skin is the situations
you walk through as a street
that has the highest accident rate
in this state"

no one lives *on* the earth,
the house is surrounded.
some think complaining to a cop
proves their innocence,
there's no point to prove.
the present is a pimple you pop
& it keeps coming back

a train of open box cars passes,
a character is going to jump on one of them.
whether he's the protagonist or primal urge
has a lot to do with how fast the train is going.

WHEN DESIRES BECOME DESCRIPTIONS

It's easier to look out from us into me than from me into us
Unless the mind's as busy as a phone without call waiting.
Yet the nut can no longer find pleasure in the shell,
Gentle as wishful thinking, that kept it from being bitten.

Do I have to become the apple that can't spoil
The whole bunch (even though it's the basket they sit in)
To sing what can't be spoken about? The screen window
Lets in light and air, but blocks the bugs who

Would kill the ones who creep in through a crack
In the wall of the flat where I await a lacklustre
Personal letter unless I'm taking up an enticing
Abstract lemma, kind of a poor man's version of a celebration

Of willessness disguised as a lament for loss of control,
A car trying to catch up with the Horizon where everything's
Condensed on a Friday night filled with teenagers who
Wished they were adults who wished they were teenagers.

Then I'm seen abandoning the car without even putting
The key in the ignition, dousing the fire because
Only the kindling had lit. But if you're here, we're
Speaking to a mind that tries too hard to flesh out

A heart that seems to precede it like a backdrop
Moving slower than the scurrying trees in the foreground.

AFTER LONG CONVERSATION

I get greedy. So summer and winter
Embrace leaving autumn's room temperature
In the dust like a jockey thrown from
A horse that, lighter, went on to win
The race (it had no idea of) but was
Disqualified (which wouldn't have mattered
to it had it not been taken back to
the stables and discreetly shot).

As long as this is a realistic picture
I feel good enough to think life isn't
Passing me by but not so good to think
Life's not passing them by unless I plant

The bugs closer in hopes every Omniscience
Is not the Grinch in drag. And such hopes
Only seem to put consummation off
When I forget to defy logic, the death
Of logic as we defy poetry or what poetry
Threatens to be especially if not interrupted

By an urgent call from an angry friend
Who's starting once again to waken to
Her needs that aren't being met or raised
By wolves after being orphaned by decorations
In the halfway house of freedom whose time
Has come and gone and waits in the wings we
Soar on till we crash into the sore
Subject of a skyscraper we slide down
Like firemen en route to put out what
One here among us has most likely set
In hopes of making the consumption
Conspicious unless putting a key in the
Ignition is not seen deferring the high road,
At least as cozy a prison as polite pawing
On the awkward first night when we tried
To sneak through the front following
The directions we misread each time we read
For meaning. You have to do it to understand
The directions. And once you do the directions
Are useless. But we, who love to give the
Worthless a shot, even if it means sacrificing
Our center (if it's really our center, it'll
return or seem to as now it seems to leave),
Find new uses for it in finding no uses for it
Since commodification can seep into just about
Any water supply for the sake of a complication
Not picky enough to be the clumsy commercials

In the bigtop that makes the sideshow possible
Where we love each other so much our little
Skit: "Why should I clean when I don't cook?"
"You eat what I cook." "But you would've cooked

It anyway." — will be put in the past on the
Condition the past can be put in the present
And I wait for a world, a woman who won't
Call this cheating, to blow the gameboard
Of my mind as the prayer for her could
Be seen acting from desire as much as fear.

ALLOWANCE MONEY THAT IS DEATH TO YOU

Miracles are molecules only microscopes get sick of.
Loneliness is the freedom to be caught smiling
By a machine you have to kick a pigeon off to ride.
A gavel bangs and its echo is intercepted
By the cushioning of a faith while I play
The flipside to "Love The One You're With"
As if it were the enemy of love that evaporates
When you forget yourself in a sheet of sound
To numb the screams of promises we made
To pretend to put the breaking point on hold
For as long as it takes to ride west with someone
I have to catch myself to be jealous of
For purely dramatic reasons.

I hold my tongue until sanity goes on strike
And stinks up the place with saints
That threaten to dub you satan until vexed
By breathing past the treelines of martyrdom
Into the silence that's really the next poem
Unless you can stir the clouds out without the coffee
Raining up into your face on a swing casting shadows
On the stars that treat me to all kinds of strategies
With no place to go but the house that has
So many mansions no Bible can hold it
Without being burned like the butcher cover
I blow when colder than cash until cleverness
Becomes crescive en route to a storm
Between the lines of a joke that goes over
Too well in Arkansas to ever succeed from the ear.

FRAGILE BLONDE

My self-reliant veterbrae of light
is too missing in action to be a prisoner of war.
It knows no shame, is had by no name
though they, like suitors, use it as a mirror
to impress themselves with their despair
and the triumph of pain over potbellied despair
where pain becomes pleasure in the apocrypha
that streaks by, skinny, like the black bird
with orange wings we swear we saw on the bridge
from which more nameable sparrows were seen
to bathe in the furious reflection of our curious smiles
with no sighs to prop up the baggage of drought
that circles around the corpse like non-pejorative parasites
striking the set of the coffin by making it cry
in public like a traffic jam on a day so beautiful
sacrifice is unavoidable. Each self, even the ones
called sexist, must flourish in the concrete jungle
of collage that's getting too big for its unisex britches
where everything's a mask but immortal abstractions
that can not be staged without sensurround, whispers,
burps and questions created equal to the task and trough
as if each second is a sabbath kept holy by holes I am
until you halo me in a catalogue that contains us only by becoming
unglued in the prelude that swells the bank of the song
you could say I'm commissioned to write all night
by a constancy who wants to see me small, ground me
against a wall to shuffle the deck of ceremony out of fear of
the dreck I escaped by the scruff of my neck, alone, in tennis,
whose nerves would have me so kept and pointless
in peacetime until the suitor dressed up with no
place to go, the clothes blowing from the line, demand
I shoplift them and, mutually empowered, we
are imprisoned in a sitcom, singing remakes
of the simplicity signed on the dotted line of
seen-through hooplah, though secret to those
who have a stake in the snake conventions,
the smoke filled rooms of the garden party

about to be fired, in anticipation of that sacred moment
that bosses us around if we're willing.

FISH STORY

The things we see our reflections in
have no time to reflect and are not things.
A reflection is seen. Of what? Not me
until I comb my toupe, am thrown for
a loop I can only see when still.
I am never still, but my shed skins are.
I put on the snakeskin suit
and leave the driving to them. It's cute
to be lead around by the dead.
I must be a deadhead. But even the dead
die and I refuse to go phishing
and so become fish. It is my sign.
Better to be a big fish in a shrinking pond
than those with rods and hooks.
I can no longer eat and must be eaten.
The drought makes me an easy catch.
As the hooks sent from the boats sink in,
I notice the fishers too busy seeing their reflection
in what's left of the water to look me in the eyes.
Well, you might as well cook me.
But after being photographed alongside of me,
you throw me back. Afraid of what I'd do
inside of you?

"LIBERAL BESTÉ"

Once upon a time, I, there was a moment.
Lovely and anxious and forever (shhhhh)...
and moment said:

You know, I try to do my liberal besté,
but sometimes, something, comes out in jest...I,
realize the only person I should have this,
running commentary with, is me.

If I am the truly open mind I claim,
why, do I feel, today, the same?
Is a moment of
shhhhh...offa sound...offa-ever (*inhale/exhale*) forever...
...please, close your mouth.
Close to open too far, open ears,
close ONE hath, only TWO quarter-pieces of blue,
WHY did I ever trust you? fly 'shoo...

A single eighth's analogies.
A Brubeck spiral's subtlety.
Ring a void of vapid null.
A nihilistic solo, please.

Suck off this electric blue guilt.
Tie this protection by a pier sifting stilts.
Where the pool issa sol-breeze ism
offa gold gilt pheasant
a delicate prick...
and nothing's left, but a dream.

Tie this kaleidoscope heart by a moor
and then a wall of love.

Amor, and then some mür of singe of
'lectric tinged, of blistered twinge, of
moments of moments of brutes maintained
and maimed and claimed and blamed
for all collapse and all defaults and all of all, in all, why all
did you flip, me, just like that?

Have you seen my four sides?
Can you choose your own thrill?
If-I-(chicka-chicka)
don't-(chicka-chicka)
you-(chicka-chicka)
will.
So-why-(chicka-chicka)
don't-(chicka-chicka)
you-(chicka-chicka-CHILLLLLLLLLLLLL!!!!!!)

You knew what bones to push, to twist,
that cafeter first, and fires a fist.
Oh moment, you fall swickly, liftly, flist-breeze down.
A goose fitz-bew by blissful-briss. YOU, sir, is-I,
IS-SLAMM-MAIC gorgeous tile,
A RACKSHAW RICKSTER STEAMS THE NILE!
A floating baby-hood's disgrace.
Rabbi Rickster sprays the mace.

Pull the splinter
and save the bone...
Baby head, ingested-tested-toster-tone,
to Dizzy, blown, phobe.

Cinammon sacs of lovely Bop.
Dizzily flip the clouds on top.
Scalloped falcon Peregrine,
I, tail, once upon a time...

...there was a moment,
lovely and anxious and forever, shhhhhhhhh...

"LET'S GO SWIMMING IN THE KEY OF C"
(Excerpt)

Give me an hour, for tide-sakes, plank-ton, foam-swash, sifted
shores. Oh, there are so many waves I'd like to wish you with.
Tell me a story...but wait, let me, you see, I wanna go swimming
in the key of C. I wanna be playing to symphonia's nymph
Manets, float-illy, watery-lilly chalet. Atlantis recounters a por-
poise attack and I wait. There are only so many undying breaths
left in this pole of a tad. Po' little crabbin' it'll only be a matter
of time. And time is reached where there are no coiled references
to hair-dos penumbra-both up and down below-numbra! As
dark as your witch bades you come in good fortune. As short as
your locks let you swooze through salacious engineers of ribbons.
Umbilical ribbons. Patrinnical trimming. A quarter-inch of
sound-stuffs, particled rough audicals, bound oracal. Does tena-
cious tease meet me for a drink while lizards discuss publishers
past? Ohio's presents? Happy the holi-DAY-O, do I-know,
more than I should of Peninsula-Mio? Sure I do! Do she know?
NO! S C A L E S L O P P Y pour honesty's froth as
your lips spill over into bribery-self-taught. Sneak an hour, here
& there as the macho noon gets longer and westward. High rise
you get out of me, pity you won't. Promised a 'dezvous, just get
a deja. Vous? Yeah, couldn't resist. That's why I hugged in the
ocean of thorned horses. Unbridled and slowly, unthere. I don't
want to hurt you, so don't hold me with slender, beautiful
promises that cradle my swoon. I'll hold it for...I'll hold you as I...
I'll hold it as long as I can. Aztec-land-lioness begotten, for
muir consumed, by breath exhumed...HOLD IT! Your breath,
under-water, in the sea of C-siousness. Stream of nonsciessness.

"INDIAN HAND POEM"
(this is a story told with hand movements)

I met an Indian in the park.
Not that kind of Indian, this kind.
He was feeding olive-pits to a little squirrel.
I offered to help,
and he turned into a little girl.
Not that kind of little girl, this kind.
She started to read pages from her diary.
She read:
"I saw Ptolomé yesterday.
He said don't do that in front of me.
I think I'm in Love with him."
I offered to help her, and she turned away.
Not this way, that way.
I ran after her,
and caught you.
You danced around me...not this kind of turn...

I kissed your breath. I kissed your spirit.
Splinters of sugar cane down from your eyes.
Painfully. Effortlessly.
I kissed my tears from your cheeks.
They tasted sweet.
I started to itch.
I opened my eyes...
and I was wearing a red dress made of green cactus needles.
And my insides felt like they were swelling up
with a thousand eyeballs.
I started to cry.
A clown walked by, looked at me, smiled, and started to cry.
I offered to help.
And the clown, turned into a cloud.
And the cloud settled down around me and told me a story.

And the cloud said:
"When angels *fall in love,*
they place their halos over each others' chest
and let their hearts fall through.

They look down and watch,
as their hearts form a cloud around them.
They embrace.
The cloud you're in, is the heaven I feel when I'm with you.
And if the skies should be sad with you.
Let me be the one
to catch the raindrops from your eyes."

So I said:
"Well, what do you mean by that?"

And the cloud drifted away.
Taking the rain within, and letting the wind come in.
And my eyes, my eyes could feel the tease of the breeze.
And I could hear heaven scream and silence dream so sweet.
And I didn't hurt anymore.
And the cloud had left a jar filled with eyes.
Eyes that had cried a thousand lives.
And everywhere I moved, they followed.
I opened the jar,
and heard the most amazing sounds.
A little girl walked towards me and started to sing.
I started to feed her eyeballs.
And she lost her sight.

If love takes mistakes and makes them love,
why can't I find my cloud?
Why is it always the sun?
Always the sun?
Never the dark?
Never the clouds?

A MORIR SOÑANDO – TO DIE DREAMING...

is the name of a drink from the islands, made of orange juice and milk
and it tastes *SO HEAVENLY* – that you Die Dreaming.
And I have...many times.
And this dead...not having passed through my lips...never touched my sleep...my break.
Mi dia speaks...in *tok-tok-tok / tok-talkin' that tickly-talk*...and I recall...
I always thought the name of the drink was, "MARIE Soñando-MARIE Dreaming"...
"Marie" sounds like "Morir."
Marie sounds like death.
Marie maybe makes the sounds of death, Marie...
Marie maybe died dreaming – a sunspot – a large room – breathing at the shins – recall...
Waking? walking away? – leading me? from me?
Exposed? Short Red Pants. Cafe Picaresque Con Leche..."*Marie, esta soñando?*"
(carra...wha...carra...sling...sarra...fwa...ch!)
A hopeful scenario – I have dyed...my milk orange...many times.
Marie – In Steeped Arrival – In Short Red Pants...makes many sounds.
Many Chopefull Mellifluous Jelly Freshtables!
Envision Enventual stripping of gears **(legm! croint! reaks! ph!)**
Implossibility Recognized. Geometric Mantra-yana.
                                          ...I dream of sleeping but I might die...
                                          ...I dream of sleeping but I might die...

Cucaracha Piston. Maybe-There-Baby-Dot breaks my plane...
Diagonally Static.
Stasis Wavers Pulpitation.
A.Citric.Bovine-charge...Grabs my eyehold
from across the, "What're-You-Lookin' -At?" Intake. Ocean to Spoon. Implode Motor One.
...drink a dream and have some fun...
...I see it's my left side that's left me...
...earlier than expected...

Raw Systems Lick. Bother Boil. Flush Glue.
Luid Icidy. Coloura Saint Sancuben.

I'll arrive by daylight, cry when I leave her.
I'll cable my morning, tell her I love her.
Toast her delicious,
Con leche, con puro.
Un cuerpo carabaiño del dia,
A bodyspeak of music of day.
I'll call you bovino-little round sunshine-pulp me a *moo-mi amor...esta soñando?*

TIGHTROPE CURVES ACROSS EQUATOR

Came here looking for
horizon, found only interruption —
calling out indifference, screaming out
mis
    calculation and big feet...tripping

                over screams

Horizon has orange belt, holding night
to sky, staring me in
mouth — scattered verticals remind
me of my too-thin demeanor, the
razor sharp blankness I call on —
in times of uncertainty

        I was unstable
        until I thought I knew what
        balance was —

Familiar pity swallows
an anvil, throwing this angularity
off — my weight is a number I swallow
every morning at breakfast
When I'm done with my mouth I clean
it's edges and look forward
to it's daily catch
My mouth is a fishing void
attracting larger cracks
than my smile, when I close it shut,
before I trap — it's corner curls
a distant crawl...until I recognize
it's bait —

              — I catch — then, I
                clean — then, I quarter
                with slivered edge...the liar inside

Who am I — to corner my
instability with balance — who

am I trying to filet, who's halo
have I borrowed for this torment — easier
to rely on distance, when the mirror's just
a little too clean —

It's ocean that I scream into
Ocean that I am — a scream
into a screamin' each other out — am'ing
The i I am — and I remain

Buzzed into my morning smile
Shut into my slivered lie — at every
number — I stop — I lift my arms
Walking
Across tethered mile — I'm a tightrope
looking down
at you looking up at me no ine
holds my either end
flat
like faceless smile

A PAGE FROM THE FLICTIONARY OF DEAFENINGTION

My sweethren, as yeu floominstasis throughout yeur wordxixtence, how woult yoo have forseeked apleasurenoon-perious-erience which cold plester reincantation anew alife agiver to slay the death of destiny ty live the life of windfamy purely oun grounds in vlertigotinous levesls unachieved heretofore bow the maxistanchions in the landscape of the you-misphere of intellect,. My brethren, yeo have tesseled upon a warm fact! If indeed indexi pleeds anew guarrano, within normal krens of course, where does will play the cantor of excellence? Whichfore and towards howhoom do the foliages within the Flictionary Of Deafeningition concooket misers crooked trunies? In not my way I as seen yuo ti not mail the stammer tren O' postage froom cottages wren wickles blerrr potatting frennjimm,. Don;t acquiese potential potage for a mere rapier-swift at ship-frinze. Don;t settle', In point of factin; manny have men toon' et gifting have women trells to jike, worrycurls to niu, fillomew tomoo, vera bihffene chillu m'kiss. My sistren, yeu quate secre migh cretions, undeniable in beaute. Yeo flay ere unop tressma, await agiver alifing, millnest tries ta suol o ion. L. I reamen flost, pore floaah, kin s, nore yes. My peoplen, th strato gives mist ty meanin, mere need ty giving, foggance askance living, yeu niss ty flo tis hills, o'er the youmisphere of intellect,. tas n yu,. and gusp breth diip, my sweethren, deep.

BIZZARRO WORLD ADRIFT

Horrible
Such darkness bitter envy
Just horrible
Mirror Id
Swollen self broken
Me
A chance
A brainscape sung
A mountainside...
If I had
If I could
I'd flip sorrow once over the sun
Four
Into millenia — & next week too
My glow would generate stars
Into galaxies people would carry
Inside...

Horrible
Such honesty
So k-zerrible
Mirror World
So blind
Me
A burn
A spark
A playchild for half a second
You were there
An unknown instrument
The vibrate of my symphony
The where-ever   *you spake of mine, & thus also of*
                       my rant, unbeknownst to I...Aye — good
                       myre, the sleek is a tenant in THIS
                       building — unvaccumed surly, Brutish to
                       sensitoopid penses, s'penses...estoy pen-sando á'yer...

**I wonder where america gets the food
that fills america with america?
fat on america
greed working overtime why does america
prevent america from
itself? letting america think for itself is
— it seems — unamerican
them-ocracy in action,
give the people too much people-do much,
give it back to — them & o-cratics
radic nervous systems say "HOLD 'EM DOWN,
YOU WANT A MUTINY HERE?"**

Horrible truth
Such darkness bitter hope
Mirror Id comma D
Unshaven self
Sailing...
If I did
If I am
My own ship to sail
To mutinize, then...
Noggin' be my captain
Skinsail be my
Bodyship
Bloodrule

*guide us through oceans' eyre
not one can claim us – speak up, fine selves
no one steers – no one invades...
may we discover, another part of we
in the everyday – alwaysday – foreverday
tis the same ocean – we pass – each others
a bit at a time – a little more each day*

from *SONNETS OF A PENNY-A-LINER*

$6.16

I want to love, and to be left alone,
I want to do what I want, I want
my time filled up with tasks, I want
to have friends, can't stand
to see anyone, I want the sky
to drench me with light, the sun
to be blotted out, I want to live live live
I wish I was dead,
my possessions are my contradictions
and all I've never owned,
today I walk from work in the snow
knowing these tricks are how I know me
and they are never going away; then why deny
violence at the core of my gentleness?

$6.30

I'll never write another poem
which means it's time to start again
like a face that's blank at the window
is not a moon but the way
I have nothing left to say
is the single ground of my poetry
Choke me, for once, insatiable air
you are an empty mimic
feeding on the genius
of my hollow solemn swaying, the moon is not
baying at me, I'm not saying
all it may not mean, at least
my stumbling is over
now that words have left

$6.44

Never mind, the mirror doesn't see
what no one would ever look into it,
I tripped, thought of ways
to not be here like a callous air
redundant, leap me against the sullen
quiet of the cultured dumb
my jagged piano shatters, a trumpet raves
through another lost version of ends,
I've sipped painted lies, been a survival
in all the obvious days, my death
will not find gloom, money
is not a reason to work,
poems are not work, news
is not a way of writing

$6.58

Swing back and forth, streets
are jumping like men into pits
of thoughts — they wished they didn't have
my city — a secret
agent of unnamed thrills,
it escapes,
work is filled with forms
that do not need to happen,
mornings I steal laughter
before the legions start making their charges
We still live in ancient Rome,
I will trade my armor and sword
for the latest computer system
and see who says there's a difference

$6.72

I'm on the train of seasoned
cacophony, past the edge
of untranslated walls, which jut
across my back, to suspend

one trips to the snack bar,
whosoever made this food
hangs me from a buttress, I go
so far as lights rush past
the winds like dreams I've forgot,
am better off a singe
or fragile fabric, talking to streets,
resisting repugnance
in quarries where silence dies
more violent than these tracks

$6.86
Bliss finds me in corners, on the verge
of sleep, rift in the day
of tasks, of drains and training,
freefall along roads
of dubious disguises, a solemn blank
that is my error not mine, to watch
slips out, here and not am,
however long there is to go
it never adds up, I grin
like a hidden number, the secret
told to everyone to be
if they will only miss it,
I won't come up when I go down
until it glows and each one sieves

$7.56
You'd think the sky would be easy to find
but I can struggle with anything,
poets on the radio, brief meetings
with nothing at all, Sunday night,
America in your cities of power
I blame my soul for shrinking,
but I will be a caravan
and not a desert, jewels will grow
even from wasted pity
and torn connections, in hills

where mouths will cry for a roof,
I remembered a poem today on the subway
for loving the love that escapes us
and anger which ruptures all quiet

$7.70
Some cities stop in snow
others are colder and keep on going
this is my life and to see
it frittered away is not a tragedy
but unlike a graph of the fall of empires
you don't always feel the borders crumble
each time there's dust in your hand
from some misdirection that flails in the night
when temperatures suddenly change
and rain that falls is not the snow
one was sure of having,
bite the missed chances that dream
in the years, press
your foot in the ground as it melts

$8.12
I want to be a crease
in well-laid plans and slowly
crack to bring them down,
I hate all doctrines, abstractions
my grandness is my bed
that sits on the ground, the chipped plaster
of my walls, irrelevant noise and the telephone
cord I wrap around me and laugh,
I will never give in if I have to be
one of the killers, or dull, or strapped
to responsible nightmares, choked on use,
I want to grow like a cheap melodrama
bursting its commercial redundance,
like a painting whose torment is sunshine on a hat

$8.26
If I was alone in the house
I would say more than the grocer's delay
and wind at the windows and winter
and what I do for money, but I
am surrounded by parrots, and what they speak
has no more to do with more
than a wall has tails, which this one does,
if I think a little longer
I'll tell myself I'm here, that songs
are really more graceful than slick
Have you seen the latest feature
of debt, of torn down curtains,
have you missed each stray beginning
or seized the moments that seized you?

$8.40
Work I suppose had meaning once
but wind churns under my hands,
magic I believe is mechanics and a trial
and dozens of silent displacements,
I wanted words to be
a surgery of aesthetic desire
despondent or dancing, yellow, a face on my wall
hanging round and fat in the grin
of bad taste, music in a minor
key of shadows and drifting, grimness and candles
different from the institutes
of quiet healthy death,
at war all the time with the culture
of any solid grasping, any wealthy cage

$8.54
What is it that keeps me
half owning myself and half
scaling the heights of what is lost
in crannies that others

tell me it's possible to buy,
today is for sale a dollar a drink
I laugh at those who run ships
onto rocks of cash
and never heard the sirens, one step
and another and this is life
it's said when living is stopped
by border patrols, hide the shining
sieves on my hands, pour
the water in, spending like a corporation

$8.68
The eyes of the spider are on me,
Hoffman in his salamander dreams
plagues me in the grass, in circumscribed dramas
of my soul among milk crates, and my late
twentieth century shabby romanticism
Don't ever tell me being practical is good
when snakes are singing in my ears
of all I think that never will happen
in these sarcophagus nights, corporations are sprouting,
I love the rats that tumble buildings
in the final earthquake of six-packs
drinking is structural, the flame
that glows in my sneakers
lights my way at the gatepost, you three-headed dogs!

$8.82
My brain is a blank afternoon
at the end of a century of lies,
the hollow thumping is my
blood against fences,
the random flinging of my hands
composes a reason for living
as though I'm painting a hidden sidewalk
only my enemies walk on
until they flower like dancing

which I do in my room all alone
with shadowed lamps and walls that say
this wreck is building the days,
clamor of a dubious underworld
that sings of my defeat

$8.96
Let winds sweep down from the arctic
I sit here smoking illusion
overworked, delaying the doom
like a grim Romantic faker
who doesn't work for bureaus
of news and lies and mannerism
Sweep me from plates
of destiny, I'm one of the hordes
who go unheeded in poverty
of access to stars, and huddle
against hours and tasks
that bury like graves
of complacent desperation, I am an eagle
who paints the fences, I am secret and waiting

$9.10
At the cost of all depth
of respect the travesty is yours
like a flaming ideogram
of the flatter portions of your head,
I want to be connected
to waterfalls and lions
but my family all are preachers
of doom, branches spread
even to my socks, for ten generations
the stories will return
I sit behind a desk
balancing accounts, swimming
in unclear bankrupt halls
bringing reports to the Bureau of Hope

Elizabeth Willis

UNDER THE ARC / of disaster

blue bodies of dauphins

the starred wheel
    (spurred)

the direction of light
    (imperative)

goes I   To be flying

also would be the sensation of a wick burning

They lit their bodies like wicks, from the skin

inward   (It was childhood)   wanting to tell how I saw

myself: dying   a glass poured back against

pink wrists

tragedy of shaved heads (shaven)

To be both larger and smaller than one

is   The dark branches of a God

A sense of the universal   (Tulips in a white hand

One would notice this time the off-green of the stems)

What goes on in the other room is of no concern and therefore

no promise   The tale of the divine

a mark on the wall

We hear its wings flap when we sleep   A late dinner

with one light on and the breathing going on

around one telling one where one is: rather a map to

this lit spot   Outlines of: finely grained

and what is no longer eaten: one can after all

never be too soft   too

ready for that water in the crease of a hand

A figure appears just out of vision but approaching

in the endless way of a move South or a meal

postponed   The word tarmac arching

whippoorwilled light   Chooses chaos or to winter

deep in the body

The figure of descent is no more than

the sensation of opening the mouth

That something could /the precipice/ slit

friction like a skin, body lose its body to one

absolute seam   Would count its hard losses

as teeth of new corn, the salt and its savor

Therefore the direction of light

is imperative, seen only from above

They are fields of star (that foreign)

when they touch absolute black

they begin to light up

BETWEEN THE ACTS

Between all the versions of "what I want to say is"
a row of schoolbusses at the back of a drive-in off the rail line.

A breath "drawn" or taken, meaning
even to be is to use up
something.   Pond lilies brown on their stems
would be all in one skillet, the abandoned
borders of hydrogen.   Earth endlessly

flattened at the backs of our eyes
wades guilt like a narrow passage.

At will we show bones through skin
or flounce the word "rumpus" to mean
the trouble one causes on one's own, plane from which

bombs scatter like Havana cigars
hands flutter like candy wrappers.   Dangerous

she said.   Meaning
you are beautiful.
Dangerous
blackens one arm's belly.

It was love as a taste in the mouth,
a shape of trees laundry infringes.

Road that doesn't disappear or wind but hovers at a surface
we try to hold down and (not) see the other side of.
This, and this quietest word. A pale eye.
(I want to enter here, my whole body.)

Tries to conceive it, clothes falling — or parentheses?

Roll it backwards in the reeling light.
The nearness of shoulders, how all is
offered up as if on the back of a dying horse
or center of a light-struck field.

The way "three winters" signifies equally
as three Havana cigars, three antelope striding
down the streets of Laredo.

Windows open to other windows, turn you out
scene as much as seeing. This tick

tick down
the grid of our lives
the notches on walls
the space between beds
between our long teeth
and final hands
closest set of crossed eyes

scattering lights of where, of when Delilah
tried to teach me to walk like a gazelle over the Rio Grande

bricks ticking at our soles
tick and tick of shed light

we have opened the box
shelled buildings with our insatiable hands
fallen forward and against
the stolen meals and borrowed clothes

tick of our growing

buttons like elbows rattling
like furniture, meaning
time and what could never be time
enough for bodies

to descend on each other like lists.
You for instance are last week's
red-skinned potatoes, this week's Ida-spuds
and Rome windfalls and all the fishsticks you can imagine.

left hand: hollow hollow o
right hand: also it was the series of embraces on the Syracuse
platform.

Crisis?   there is no crisis
but tick of the pen
of teeth ticking
the shelled busses
lilies in parentheses, cupped hand of a lens

tiles ticking past
where we, real, wobble

no crisis
but of the iris in
containing light
crisis is the blue mountains' blueness
or the ankle in each step

further, there

is no crisis
but of the iris in containing

JORDAN (H-YRDN)

(i)   *the names of the lovers are entwined in a garden*

no me
who has no name

right itself

as in
the omission of one letter

———

all things turn

to the eye of the goat
our father

And to the eye our mother

All things/ turn in the eye

as by a strange hand
taken *down*

———

Notice then the further inversion.   *Who are you/ you who have entered /*
The asphalt radiant// Had been "garden"/ or a desert moved.   Azrael
contained that letter / in the rib of his mouth.

———

who but you)

captive by the face of the fire

ash came// *ash-sham*
a kingdom

-verted in the midst

the woundedness

buoyant in (a world /
the dream in Rabbah:

walls grew up like flames.

———

(ii)

      canceled

a fabrication or fabric

    (She was in love

with the mother, with Thetis)

Tiomat / the coast engulfed her

or "ate its young"

Nothing (whatever was forbidden
            the forbidden god

was ruin, *mafi*

dolphin or the mourning scarf she

took from the brink

———

where the lady is

found : "released"

comes again to the hierophant

— the magus —

O, sire is that
you   is that

possible, faltering

but absorbed in her light

the hive / a tomb

in it:
a daemon no less

deflected, no less angelic

were it Eurydice

fallow in the sun

her pace (fallen)

the gatekeep (Egyptian)

as *that which existed between*

which tore from them

———

(iii)

At Amra: Andromeda with spread arms

To the east of "river"
                second circle is Cygnus
"escarpment"
            and the Dolphin

First-known claiming heaven

there as here the color
blasted into Christ
∎
A new voice (holden)

"as in the former years"
the Straight road
whilst we walk: sweet spring
                black iris

to drink of the river: Sihor or Sidon
∎
too strong for the vessel
that *Allat* and a jealous stone/

without walls
was "outside" or in unity

of a flower we/ lap or give her
∎
Polydictes: confounding the tongues

Polydectes, who 'receives many'
the outer covering of the flower
∎
pearls *the fortune of*
the law a beacon, thinking back

was the desert
where the iris spoke
■
here the cold is beginning

The picture was not the many receiving
pearls from the wise but bringing them

"Sea creatures with human heads"
brought them to shore in their mouths
■
But we all, with open face
beholding as in a glass

his "Read"/ "I cannot read" crossing
"speak" or "write" in that place

who touched my mouth broke the band

—————

(iv)

"roses or a rose city"

damascq: ash-sham
a linen hand tampered with

where one was (a skirt
traces the escarpment

from Taurus
to the Pleiades/ a hem

of possession and retrieval

below earth and below
the sea

If the river were in flames
a dove also
was a form of commerce
and a lion existed like two
cypress trees beyond which the City
lit

In walls
          a city without border/
from the edge of that rose
          three worlds fell away

fraction of stone
in the eye of God

first half of the sentence is lost

Qeys / Queyes
mother or a city of the lover

Between the north and the southern Karnak

The sea encompasses me, encompasses my Book.

of "increase" as of "deliverance"

It was their blessing that they were lost

and so retained each other:
Qeys and Lubna at the tomb

In Enoch's city / a bead game (of memory)

of Mary / of the rose.

She conceived like a mare, by the wind.

At the opening of the Mouth / all the apertures

filled her, Mara
who remains "empty" / Maia the midwife

bearing / to revel and reveal.

———

(v)

sometimes it is named "tree" and sometimes "sun"

It was about pearls, the picture of the fish.

Arthemis/ *samakah* deep in this river

or a hillside against white wings
searching the mouth

healing the sunless one
mutilated and adorned

'to be removed'

from the Taurus down/ strikes the rose
into Karnak of Thebes.

Thad Ziolkowski

from *OUR SON THE ARSON*

Floating
in the problem

which no longer functions as an image,
the home of the free

is the light of watching
the light

of writing people
walking in the street.

It does what I think is
today, depending

from a tether
of thought about it.

One is all
things at once.

Names for the baby are
not the baby, but no one recalls how

it all adds up
in the space provided

in the end
of our having forgotten that

once upon a time
everywhere present

we made it
then made it

pound a stake through the heart
of that intention.

———

The gun went "click"
in the class picture. The sun
sank slowly in the west
his friend left

for the field we live in, well
begun, half done. The
words

"we"
mean

the Bank.

———

The remains of what authorities say
are the man and the woman
who lived above the video store were found
in the smoldering debris of the building
by searchers using dogs. There is sun
only on the avenues. Stop

and watch for my signals. You are in grave danger. I am
disabled, communicate
with me, for you
are in grave danger, too.

Unless it is itself
in flames, part of me
explains, a fly

can light on an ash, by the whole heavens, and remain
a formula, scaffolding for what
was to have been more
scaffolding.

———

Month, day,
year, firemen

breathing
in the firehouse, anything.

Anything may function as an example
of something that it is

scooping out the top of
in order to move more

freely there.
Just the check

please. There
would always be a time

and a situation. North
is not up

but a moment of
what for

no one
it

intervenes
in

———

I wave back from
all things being equal

to the accident of their appearance
it seems to follow

as a result of laws of state
other than the state
imposing the laws

on the member
and illustration of the more
general class
of the no longer possible

waters
connecting the dots
on an oak lashing against
the two
sides of the question

————

Specter gesticulating to itself and to
someone also absent

hence total
as versus a given whole with its gently

hemorrhaging fears of what not having a question
left might mean

to the even flame
of its generality breath

boils down to the chain
between steps

and their taint

of intent which is also

anywhere
light stomachs

the rest
and rock

breaks scissors before
they can cut

paper that would have
covered it

per the elders and the law
that hid from us what happened

to us as we
were the world we

slowly fled with the coin
of that realm

and our son
the arson

———
———

Becoming ate

the bridge away.

One future, beaten to death

in the Fountain of Unlikeness,

names names outside

of you

and the flowers are perfect.

There's an interval between the flowers

but they're perfect.

If there were others.

———

All my life one
source said though
it and how

the terms what they might
if at first
seeds thank you for
not I
don't know but
try me

———

The world in

which bodies die

showers possible

going-away

presents.

But Dad

sounded sad

inside the coin.

———

Because there is no mother

there is no father

and so no mother either

and therefore no father

because no mother

or father

            no and

         no and no and

            or either

———

Thank you thank

whom, tender

limit of seeking

sought, has

been arrived at

here, may X

mark the spot

impossibly and I

pass in and out

———

I'm with

you in

one of

us it

not we

built from

a kind

of thinking

of one

another

under

another name

omitted

among other things

real

———

Where others

protected by

the stars

upon a spot

and suns, go

as if an axle

I've known

to wrap

without

or rip

that sign

North

(after Dickinson)

———

An open totality hung by a mob

to produce change

the feeling has surpassed

qua sky

folded in half

then in half again

from Terminal A

through the device

back to Terminal B

———

The sun, the sun

in which I lose

the ball is

inside. There,

on 31 August

1941, Tsvetaeva

took her own life.

(Continued on back flap)

Postface

That there be poetry at all would seem a virtual impossibility, even in or especially in a culture of superabundance and lack like our own. We participate in this engine, of course — the engine that governs time and divvies up space, and usually in contradiction to our needs — and poetry is just another kind of fuel or fodder for it, the self-conscious will insist. But poetry's is not the kind of energy whose commodification can lead to a place in the world of hegemonic desire, the more complete self-consciousness argues, since in order to work poetry must always keep things fluid, that is to say, must always work against a world-picture which stabilizes or legitimizes domination. And so in this book we are able to present both a "New Gate" and a fluid "river" Jordan, to borrow two figures from Garrett Kalleberg and Elizabeth Willis respectively: an "opening to concrete fields, streams, and states," and a network of words that lead to "Enoch's city / a bead game (of memory)," which might be interpreted to mean the possibility of a temporal reach and the creation of an apocryphal insertion. Against the odds and in the face of the phenomena Lisa Jarnot speaks of in her introduction, a series of intimate conversations with other persons, with language, and with time and space finds a place and hopefully is here furthered. Are the aspirations of these poets possible after all?

The work of this new generation is impressive by any standard. Most of the poets here have published a first book or chapbook, as noted in the introduction. Several of these writers — Ben Friedlander, Bill Luoma, Jennifer Moxley, Eleni Sikelianos — are already accomplished translators as well as poets: translation, that co-related art whose presence is often the measure of the depth of a poetry and the commitment of a given generation to their project. Some of these poets have already received significant critical attention both underground and in academic and poetry world institutions. Yet something of Moxley's "Ode To Protest" accrues to the stance of the poets in this book taken as a whole: "If only we had means/ then we could give light/ to meaning. But for now/ it seems royalty will keep writing/ the book on right-of-way/ and we again shall lay/ our lives by the wayside." Poetry is here the outside force whose very marginality gives it the possibility of subversiveness: it is this idea that we have been told over and over again is no longer viable, and it is this idea that the poets here would seem to wholeheartedly embrace, over and against the cynicism that would deny the existence of an alternative discourse. Perhaps such "ode to protest" is the very risk that allows a poem to be other than advertisement for its own form.

Not to say the writing collected here is otherworldly. Poets like Rod Smith and Mark Wallace critique the heart of capital, while writers like Renee Gladman, Brenda Coultas, and Hoa Nguyen plunge fiercely into the connective tissue of everyday life and immediate perception. Jordan Davis, Jeffrey McDaniel, Thomas Sayers Ellis, and Peter Gizzi explore the textures of speech, voice, and linguistic surface to arrive at a kind of maximalism which makes of that self-same immediacy a weapon; Mark Nowak, Heather Ramsdale, Mark McMorris, Susan Schultz, and Pam Rehm fashion mythic, philosophical, and emotional structures that might equally be regarded as maximal in their breadth, ambition, and beauty. How hope to categorize the linguistic effusions of an Edwin Torres or the heady tones of a Beth Anderson? All of the poets in this book describe unique and irreducible trajectories. Each writer's work makes singular demands on our attention. These attentions quicken our intelligence and pulse. Through these poetries ideologies dissolve.

Michael Palmer once said that in the shape of America the poet's overriding mission is . . . to survive. This echoes the remark of John Cage that Lisa Jarnot offers at the outset. I believe that the poets presented in this book bespeak the terms of such survival.

Leonard Schwartz
1 October 1997

Contributors

Beth Anderson was born in 1968 in Daly City, California, and lives in Providence, Rhode Island. She attended Brown University and currently works as a lexicographer in Boston. *The Impending Collision,* a chapbook of her poetry, is published by rem • press in Cambridge, England. Her poems have also appeared in *Hanging Loose, Black Bread, Arshile,* and other journals, and her essay "Imperturbable Things," on still-life poetics, is part of The Impercipient Lecture Series. She is the editor and publisher of reference: press chapbooks, an annual three-author publication.

Lee Ann Brown's book *Polyverse* won the New American Poetry Prize and is forthcoming from Sun & Moon Press. Her chapbooks include *Crush* (Leave books), and *a museme* (Boog Literature). Recent journal publications include *The Capilano Review* (Vancouver) and *No Trees* (New York City). Her work has been anthologized in *Writing from the New Coast* (o.blek editions), *Out of This World* (Crown), and *Primary Trouble,* (Talisman House) and will be included in a Nude Formalism section of a new anthology of formal poetry. Since 1989, she has been the editor of Tender Buttons press, which features experimental poetry by women. Born Friday, 11 October 1963 (Libra) near Tokyo, Japan, and raised in Charlotte, North Carolina, Brown holds an MFA in Creative Writing from Brown University. She has taught writing at Brown, the Naropa Institute's Jack Kerouac School of Disembodied Poetics, and St. John's University, and has taught filmmaking at the University of Rhode Island. She is currently an Associate of the Institute for Writing & Thinking at Bard College. From 1987-1991 she worked at the Poetry Project at St. Mark's Church in New York.

Mary Burger was born on 5 March 1963 in Canton, Ohio. She is co-editor of *Proliferation,* an annual journal of new writing, and editor of the chapbook series Second Story Books. She is the author of the prose work *Bleeding Optimist* (Xurban Press), and her writing has appeared in *Chain, mirage, Open 24 Hours, Prosodia, Mass. Ave., Situation, TINFISH,* and others. She holds a BA in English literature from Oberlin College, a MA in Creative Writing from Boston University, and a MFA in Writing and Poetics from The Naropa Institute. She has designed letterpress and offset book and journal covers for Xurban Press, *Proliferation, Superflux,* and idiom chapbooks. She lives in San Francisco.

Brenda Coultas was born 18 September 1958. She is a contributing editor to *PsaLm 151* and is the author of *Early Films* (Rodent Press). She lives in Brooklyn and teaches a workshop at the Poetry Project.

Jordan Davis was born in 1970 in New York City. He studied at Columbia University, then he edited the *Poetry Project Newsletter*. His books include *A Little Gold Book* (Golden, 1995) and *Upstairs* (Barque, 1997). He prints Goodbye Books, and with Anne Malmude, he hosts the Poetry City reading series at Teachers and Writers Collaborative in New York.

Thomas Sayers Ellis was born in 1963 in Washington, D.C. and received an M.F.A. from Brown University in 1995. A co-founding member of The Dark Room Collective, he has been published in *AGNI, Best American Poetry 1997, Boston Review, Calalloo, Grand Street, Hambone, Harvard Review, In the Tradition: An Anthology of Young Black Writers, The Kenyon Review, Ploughshares, The Southern Review,* and *The Garden Thrives: Twentieth-Century African-American Poetry*. He has received fellowships from the MacDowell Colony, the Provincetown Fine Arts Work Center, and Yaddoo; and in 1993 he co-edited *On the Verge: Emerging Poets and Artists*. His first collection, *The Good Junk*, was published in the Graywolf annual "Take Three" in 1996. He is currently an assistant professor of English at Case Western Reserve University.

Benjamin Friedlander was born in 1959 in Louisiana, and has lived in Ontario, Missouri, California, and New York. His poetry books and chapbooks include *Dim Sparse* (Coincidence Press, 1984), *A Pinfold Pentad* (Coincidence Press, 1988), *Time Rations* (O Books, 1991), *Anterior Future* (Meow Press, 1993), and *A Knot Is Not a Tangle* (Meow Press, 1995). Friedlander's collaborations include *Nagrivator* with Pat Reed (Xena Bird, 1987), *Oriflamme Day* with Stephen Rodefer (Phraseology, 1987), *Myth* with Jeff Gburek (Phobics, 1989), and *Prophecy* with Jeff Gburek (Phobics, 1992). With Andrew Schelling, he edited *Jimmy & Lucy's House of "K"* from 1984 to 1989 and *Dark Ages Clasp the Daisy Root* from 1989 to 1993. Friedlander also edited *Areas Lights Heights: Writings 1954-1989* by Larry Eigner (Roof Books, 1989), *I Am a Child: Poetry after Robert Duncan and Bruce Andrews* (with William R. Howe) (Tailspin Press, 1994), and *Collected Prose* by Charles Olson (with Donald Allen) (University of California, 1997).

Drew Gardner was born on 12 December 1968 in Princeton, New Jersey. He graduated from Bard College in 1991, and moved to San Francisco, where from 1991–1993 he co-edited *Notus*. His work has been published in several anthologies, including *Writing From the New Coast* (o.blek) and *Primary Trouble* (Talisman House). He was the recipient of Gertrude Stein Awards in Innovative American Poetry in 1993-94 and 1994-95. He is the author of The *Stone Walk* (St. Lazaire, 1991) and *The Cover* (Leave Press, 1992) and has been published in magazines such as *apex of the M, First Intensity, Five Fingers Review, Lingo, Talisman,* and *Zyzzyva*. He presently lives in New York.

Peter Gizzi was born in 1959 and grew up in Pittsfield, Massachusetts. His publications include *Artificial Heart* (Burning Deck, 1998), *Periplum* (Avec, 1992), and the chapbooks *Hours of the Book* (Zasterle, 1994) and *Music for Films* (Paradigm, 1992). His poems have been anthologized in *The Best American Poetry 1995* (Scribners), *Sixty Years of American Poetry* (Abrams), *49 + 1 Nouveaux Poetes Americains* (Royaumont), and *The Gertrude Stein Awards in Innovative North American Poetry* in 1993-94 and again in 1994-95 (Sun & Moon). In 1994 he received the Lavan Younger Poets Award from the Academy of American Poets. His editing projects have included *o.blēk: a journal of language arts* (1987-93), the international literary annual *Exact Change Yearbook* (1995), and *The House That Jack Built: The Collected Lectures of Jack Spicer* (Wesleyan University Press, 1998). He holds degrees from New York University, Brown University, and SUNY-Buffalo. In 1993-94 he was a Visiting Poet in the Graduate Program in Creative Writing at Brown University. He teaches at the University of California, Santa Cruz.

Renee Gladman, born 1971 in Atlanta, lives and works in San Francisco. She is currently completing a MA at New College of California and edits the magazine *Clamour*. Her work has appeared in *Situation, Mass Ave., No Roses Review, Superflux, Mirage,* and *Proliferation. Arlem* was published as a chapbook by idiom press. A long work, *Not Right Now,* is forthcoming from Second Story Press.

Judith Goldman was born in Panorama City, California, in 1973. She has a BA from Brown University and is currently in the Ph.D. program at Columbia University's Department of English and Comparative Literature. Her work has appeared in *The Impercipient, Arras, Object, Torque,* and *Aerial.* Her chapbook, *adversities of outerlife* was published by Object Editions in 1996.

Yuri (Riq) Hospodar was born on Hiroshima Day 1964. He has lived in Philadelphia, Boston, San Francisco, and Prague. He has had one book published, *To You in Your Closets and Other Poems* (Stone Soup Press), and has had poems appear in *New York Quarterly, Painted Bride, Samizdat,* and other magazines.

Lisa Jarnot was born in Buffalo, New York, on 26 November 1967. She attended SUNY-Buffalo from 1985-1989 where she studied with poets Robert Creeley and John Clarke. She holds a MFA degree from Brown University. Her publications include *Phonetic Introductions* (Northern Lights, 1988), *The Fall of Orpheus* (Shuffaloff Press, 1992), *Sea Lyrics* (Situations, 1996), and *Some Other Kind of Mission* (Burning Deck Press, 1996). She has edited two poetry magazines, *No Trees* and *Troubled Surfer,* as well as *The Poetry Project Newsletter.* She currently lives in New York where she is a member of the rock band Vole.

Garrett Kalleberg was born in Brooklyn in 1961. He studied art at Cooper Union and creative writing at the City College, both in New York City. His poetry

& criticism have appeared in *Mandorla, Sulfer, First Intensity, American Letters &* *Commentary* and elsewhere; *Limbic Odes* was published by Heart Hammer Books in 1997. He currently lives and works in Brooklyn, where he edits and publishes the web journal *The Transcendental Friend*. He is editing a special section on younger poets for *Talisman*.

Candace Kaucher was born in Reading, Pennsylvania, on 6 October 1960. She holds an M.A. in Creative Writing from Temple University. Currently, she co-edits the zine *Outpost Entropy* with headquarters in the Reading area. Some of her collaborative work can be found in *Synergism: An Anthology of Collaborative Writing* (Bohosi Press, 1995). Kaucher has been a recurrent contributor to *Big Hammer, The New York Quarterly*, The *Painted Bride Quarterly*, and *6ix*. Most recently, her poetry has appeared in WORC's Aloud Allowed.

Bill Luoma was born at 5:35 am on 18 November 1960 in French Hospital in San Francisco. Half of his zodiac resides in Scorpio. He grew up in the Silicon Valley during its orchard phase. He was educated at DeAnza Community College in Cupertino where he earned an AS in Chemistry and at the University of California in San Diego, where he studied classics and contemporary writing with Page duBois, Lydia Davis, Ron Silliman, Michael Davidson, Jerome Rothenberg, Charles Bernstein and Stephen Rodefer. His publications include *My Trip to New York City* (The Figures, 1994) *Swoon Rocket* (The Figures, 1996) *Western Love* (Situations, 1996), *Ode* (BoogLit, 1996), and a selection of prose forthcoming from The Figures. *My Trip to New York City* was translated into French as *Mon Voyage a New York* by Juliette Valery and Emmanuel Hocquard. His visual poems have appeared on the covers of The *Archive Newsletter,* The *Impercipient, Object, Balance Sheet,* ®, *Ground Air,* and *The Poetry Project Newsletter*. He currently lives in Honolulu, working as a technical writer.

Kimberly Lyons grew up in Chicago, Illinois. She lives with her husband, poet Mitch Highfill, and their son Jackson in Brooklyn. She is the author of several chapbooks: *Strategies* (Prospect Books, 1993), *In Padua* (St.Lazaire Press, 1991), *Rhyme the Lake* (Leave Books, 1994), and *Oxygen* (Northern Lights International Poetry, Brooklyn Series, 1991). *Mettle,* a collaborative, limited edition with images by artist Ed Epping was published by Granary Books in 1996.

Jeffrey McDaniel was born 3 July 1967 and grew up in Philadelphia. He has read his work in National Poetry Slams and on National Public Radio. He has been published in *Ploughshares* and in *The Best American Poetry 1994* (Scribners) and is the author of *Alibi School,* published by Manic D Press in 1995. A new book, tentatively titled *Bad Pilgrim Room,* is scheduled for publication soon. He lives in Hollywood, California.

Mark McMorris was born in Kingston, Jamaica, in 1960 and has long resided in the United States, first in New York, and then in Providence, Rhode Island. His poetry appears under four titles: *Palinurus Suite* (paradigm, 1992), *Figures for a Hypothesis* (Leave, 1995), *Moth-Wings* (Burning Deck, 1996), and *The Black Reeds* (U of Georgia, 1997). With Ward Tietz, he created and performed *Accompong*, a performance installation and sound poem, at the 1996 Geneva Arts Festival. His fiction has been anthologized in *Ancestral House: the Black Short Story in the Americas and Europe* (Westview, 1995). McMorris holds degrees from Columbia and Brown and currently teaches at Georgetown University in Washington, D.C.

Jennifer Moxley was born in San Diego, California in 1964. She now lives in Providence, Rhode Island where with Steve Evans she edits *The Impercipient*, a lecture series. She is the author of *Imagination Verses* (Tender Buttons, 1996) and two chapbooks, *The First Division of Labour* (Rosetta, 1995) and *Enlightenment Evidence* (Rem•press, 1996). Her translation of the French poet Jacqueline Risset's *The Translation Begins* was published by Burning Deck in 1996.

Claire Needell was born in 1965. Her book *Not A Balancing Act* was published by Burning Deck in 1993, and *Migrations* will appear soon from T$_2$ press. Her works have appeared in *LVNG*, *Talisman*, *Poetry New York*, and elsewhere. She lives in New York City.

Hoa Nguyen was born in Vietnam on 26 January 1967 on the night of a full moon in Leo, year of the Fire Horse. She was raised in the United States in the Washington, D.C., area. She earned a MFA in Poetics from New College of California. With WritersCorps in San Francisco, she taught creative writing to inner-city youth for several years. These projects included ceramic murals, public performance, youth reading events, and two citywide youth anthologies. She currently leads creative writing classes under the auspices of Small Press Traffic in San Francisco and New College of California. Her work has appeared in such journals as *Mike and Dale's Younger Poets, Prosodia, Gas, Open 24 Hours, Chain,* and *Proliferation.* Her awards include the Zora Neale Hurston Award for Summer Study at Naropa and a grant from The Fund for Poetry. Her first book, entitled *Hood,* is forthcoming from Buck Down Books. She currently lives in Austin, Texas with her husband, the poet Dale Smith, and their two cats, Taz and Tummba.

Mark Nowak was born on 17 December 1964 in Buffalo, New York. He holds a MFA in Creative Writing from Bowling Green State University and is an assistant professor of humanities at the College of St. Catherine-Minneapolis, where he teaches courses in folklore and writing. He is the founder/editor of *Xcp: Cross-Cultural Poetics* (http://www.stkate.edu/xcp/) and the editor of Theodore Enslin's *Selected Poems* (National Poetry Foundation). Nowak's first collection of poems & "micro-ethnographies," *Revenants,* is forthcoming in the "Open Mouth Poetry

Series" (Heat Press, Los Angeles). He is currently at work on a full-length ethnographic study, tentatively titled *In Heaven There Is No Beer: Fr. Frank Perkovich and the Iron Range Polka Mass.*

Heather Ramsdell grew up in northeastern Massachusetts. She received her education in visual art from The Cooper Union and in writing from the City College of New York. Her poems have been published in *Talisman, Sulfur,* and *American Letters & Commentary.* Her book *Lost Wax* was one of the manuscripts selected in the 1997 National Poetry Series competition and is forthcoming from University of Illinois press in spring 1998. She lives and writes in Brooklyn, NY.

Pam Rehm was born in New Cumberland, Pennsylvania in 1967. Her publications include *Pollux* (Leave Books, 1992), *The Garment in Which No One Had Slept* (Burning Deck, 1993), *Piecework* (The Garlic Press, 1992), and *To Give It Up* (Sun & Moon, 1995).

Elio Schneeman was born on 16 October 1961, in Campo Di Statte, Taranto, Italy of American parentage. In 1966 Elio Scheeman moved with his family to New York City. In 1978, C Press published a collection of his poems, *In February I Think.* His poems have appeared in numerous publications, including *Transfer, Talisman,* and *Shiny,* and the anthologies *Nice To See You: Homage to Ted Berrigan* (Coffee House) and *Out of this World* (Crown/Random House). His first full-length collection of poems, *Along The Rails* was published by United Artists Books in 1991. He died 17 August 1997.

Susan M. Schultz was born on 10 October 1958 in Belleville, Illinois. She received a BA. in History from Yale in 1980 and a Ph.D in English from the University of Virginia in 1989. She has lived in Hawai'i since 1990 and teaches at the University of Hawai'i. She is the author of *Another Childhood* (Leave Books); *Earthquake Dreams* (Standing Stone Press), *voice-overs* (Tinfish Network, with John Kinsella), *Addenda* (Meow Press, forthcoming), and *Aleatory Allegories* (Folio Press, forthcoming). She has received three Gertrude Stein Awards in Innovative Poetry. She edits *Tinfish,* a journal of experimental poetry from the Pacific. She has also published reviews and criticism widely, and edited *The Tribe of John: Ashbery and Contemporary Poetry* (Alabama, 1995).

Leonard Schwartz was born in 1963 in New York City. His books include *Exiles: Ends* (1990), *Objects of Thought, Attempts at Speech* (1990), *Gnostic Blessing* (1992), and *Words Before the Articulate: New and Selected Poems* (Talisman House, 1997). Co-editor of *Primary Trouble: An Anthology of Contemporary American Poetry* (1996), Schwartz has also published numerous essays and translations in a variety of journals, including *Film Quarterly, Harper's, Afterimage, The Poetry Project Newsletter, Pequod,* and *The Journal of Chinese Religions,* among others. The recipient of an NEA fellowship in 1997, he lives in New York and is married to the Chinese poet Zhang Er.

Eleni Sikelianos' books and chapbooks include *to speak while dreaming* (Selva Editions, 1993), *Poetics of the X* (Rodent Press, 1995), *A Book of Ease / Unease* (collaborative work with artist Peter Cole) (San Francisco, 1996), *The Book of Tendons* (Post-Apollo Press, 1997). Forthcoming publications include *The Blue Coat* (Trembling Ladders) and *The Lover's Numbers* (Seeing Eye Books). She has contributed to *Sulfur, Grand Street, First Intensity, Exquisite Corpse*, etc. She is contributing editor to *Psalm 151* and is currently at work on translations of Jean Tortel. She was awarded a NEA Fellowship in Poetry in 1995.

Rod Smith was born in Gallipolis, Ohio in 1962. He grew up in Manassas, Virginia, where he attended Stonewall Jackson High School. Smith has spent most of his adult life in Washington, DC, where he formerly managed Bick's Books and currently manages Bridge Street Books. At Bridge Street, he has curated reading series that included such authors as John Cage, Carolyn Forché, Lyn Hejinian, and Tom Raworth. He is the author of *The Boy Poems* (Buck Downs Books, 1994) and *In Memory of My Theories* (O Books, 1996). A limited edition, *Protective Immediacy*, is forthcoming from Potes & Poets. *Object* 5 featured his "A Grammar Manikan" and *Abacus* 104 featured "The Lack (love poems, targets, flags. . .)." He edits *Aerial* magazine and publishes Edge Books.

Juliana Spahr was born on 7 April, 1966 in Chillicothe, Ohio. She lived there until entering Bard College. After that she went to graduate school at SUNY-Buffalo. She has worked in radio, in a parking garage, in a bar, in an office, and currently at the University of Hawaii, Manoa. She co-edits the journal *Chain* with Jena Osman. Her book *Response* has been published by Sun & Moon.

Chris Stroffolino was born 20 March 1963 in Reading, Pennsylvania, where he lived (aside from a 6 month stint in Washington serving on the staff of two failed presidential candidates) until he received his B.A. in English/Philosophy from Albright College in 1986. He is the author of *Incidents* (Iniquity Press, 1990), *Oops* (backyard press, 1991; revised and expanded ed.: Pavement Saw Press, 1994), *Cusps* (Aerial/Edge, 1995), *Light as a Fetter* (Situations, 1997), and *Stealer's Wheel* (Hard Press, 1998). His poetry has appeared in over a hundred journals, and his reviews and essays, mostly on twentieth-century poetry and poetics, have been widely published. He received a M.A. from Temple University in 1988 and a Ph.D. from SUNY-Albany in 1997. He currently lives and works as an adjunct professor in Brooklyn.

Edwin Torres was born in The Bronx in 1958. He has traveled with the poetry collective "Real Live Poetry" since 1993. He has received The Nuyorican Poets

Cafe Fresh Poetry Award & a years' fellowship from The Foundation for Contemporary Performance Art. His books include *I Hear Things People Haven't Really Said* (self-published 1991), *Lung Poetry* (self-published 1994), and *SandHomméNomadNo* (self-published 1997). His recording "Holy Kid" is available from Kill Rock Stars. He has published in *A Gathering Of The Tribes, The World, Cross Cultural Poetics, Long Shot Magazine, Tristeria, Sensitive Skin, Bomb Magazine,* and *Movement Research Journal.* He is a contributing editor to *Chain.*

Mark Wallace was born in 1962 in Princeton, New Jersey and raised in the Washington, DC area. He is the author of *Nothing Happened and Besides I Wasn't There* (Edge Books, 1997), *Sonnets of a Penny-a-liner* (Buck Downs Books, 1996), *Every Day Is Most of My Time* (Texture Press, 1994), *Complications from Standing in a Circle* (Leave Books, 1993), and a number of chapbooks, most recently *The Haunted Baronet* (primitive, 1996) and *In Case of Damage to Life, Limb, or This Elevator* (Standing Stones, 1996). He edits the poetry magazine *Situation* and, together with Juliana Spahr, Kristin Prevallet, and Pam Rehm, co-edited *A Poetics of Criticism* (Leave Books, 1994), a collection of poetics essays in innovative forms. He received a MA in creative writing from Binghamton University in 1988 and a PhD from SUNY-Buffalo in 1994. He currently lives in Washington, D.C., where he runs the Ruthless Grip Art Project Experimental Poetry Series, and teaches literature and writing at several area colleges, including The George Washington University, American University, and Montgomery College.

Elizabeth Willis was born in Awali, Bahrain in 1961 and grew up in and out of Eau Claire, Wisconsin. Her publications include a book-length poem, *Second Law* (Avenue B, 1993); *The Human Abstract* (Penguin, 1995), which won the National Poetry Series Award; and two chapbooks, *A/O* (o.blek editions, 1991) and *A Maiden* (shuffaloff, 1993). In 1991 she received a Thayer Fellowship for poetry and in 1994 completed a Ph.D. in English at SUNY-Buffalo. She teaches composition, literature, and creative writing and is poet-in-residence at Mills College for 1997-98.

Thad Ziolkowski is the author of *Our Son the Arson* (What Books, 1996) and *Dream Works* (Churchill's Books, 1996). He is currently writing a memoir about surfing. He lives in New York City.

Designed by
Samuel Retsov

||||||

10 pt Baskerville

||||||

acid-free paper

||||||

Printed by
McNaughton & Gunn